MASTERING *the* FOUR ARGUMENTS

The Classical Art of Persuasive Writing

Gregory Roper

New York • London

The publication of this book was made possible by the generosity of the Henry Regnery Legacy Fund at the Intercollegiate Studies Institute.

First American edition published in 2026 by ISI Books, an imprint of Encounter Books, an activity of Encounter for Culture and Education, Inc., a nonprofit, tax exempt corporation.

Encounter Books website address: www.encounterbooks.com
Manufactured in the United States and printed on acid-free paper. The paper used in this publication meets the minimum requirements of ANSI/NISO Z39.48–1992 (R 1997) (*Permanence of Paper*).

FIRST AMERICAN EDITION
LIBRARY OF CONGRESS CATALOGING-IN-PUBLICATION DATA
IS AVAILABLE
Information for this title can be found at the
Library of Congress website under the following
ISBN 978-1-64177-446-8

CONTENTS

ACKNOWLEDGMENTS

I have many people to thank for the thinking and teaching that went into this book.

First, I should thank people I have never met: Andrea A. Lunsford and John Ruszkiewicz (and their later collaborator, Keith Walters), Jeanne Fahnestock and Marie Secor, and John Ramage and John Bean (and their later collaborator, June Johnson) for saving me when I was teaching multiple composition sections a semester. Their texts gave me a practical, solid model from which to work, and more importantly have kept stasis theory alive. My aim for this book is refreshing their work and making it more accessible for a new group of students.

Next, I want to thank the students at Northwest Missouri State University and the University of Dallas who worked with me as I learned how to teach this method, helping me understand what I was doing and show them how to write clear arguments. I should also thank teachers from the Great Hearts schools in Phoenix, Arizona, and Irving, Texas, as well as teachers from the John Adams Academies in Roseville, California, who patiently allowed me to take their professional development time to introduce this method and whose comments and suggestions helped me to develop my presentation in these pages.

My colleagues at the University of Dallas have been enormously helpful. Sally Hicks, our interim dean at the time, and J. J. Sanford, then provost and now president, encouraged this work and provided me with a sabbatical in the spring semester of 2020 so I could complete the manuscript. My colleagues in the English department at the University of Dallas, especially Scott Crider, Katie Davis, Ger Wegemer, and Dave Davies, have listened to me rattle on about stasis theory for years and have shared encouragement, constructive criticism, and course materials. Eileen Gregory and Andrew Osborn generously gave me permission to use their essay prompts from Literary Tradition I, which you will see in chapter 5. When she was chair of the English department, Deborah Romanick Baldwin allowed me to present these ideas to our Writing Lab tutors and encouraged them to use these concepts in their work with students, even producing posters of the four templates. Andrew Moran, our current chair, always shows me new ways to see things I thought I had clear in my head, pokes at my foibles, and drives me to do more; his kindness, puns, and friendship have all been invaluable to me in ways he will never know. Matthew Post and Joshua Parens in their roles in the Braniff Graduate School and in founding our classical education program offered helpful support. Jonathan Culp taught me how to explain the fact/value distinction. Karen Gempel, then our amazing departmental administrative assistant, kept me organized and focused, especially in my nine years as chair, and is a wonderful friend. Our current provost, Matthias Vorwerk, helped me carve out the time from my current position to finish off the final editing of the manuscript and encouraged me throughout.

Rob Jackson, when he was with the Great Hearts schools and their Institute for Classical Education, repeatedly offered me a forum in which to work out these ideas, try them in teachers' workshops, and articulate them in print. Now having founded Classical Commons, he has insisted on the value of this project and the need for me to get this book into the hands of those who could use it. Paul Weinhold, when he was headmaster at Great Hearts North Phoenix Preparatory Academy, shared his facilities for one of those workshops and has himself offered me useful criticism. I am thrilled that he now leads our classical education program at the University of Dallas. R. J. Pestritto had me up to Hillsdale College to talk about Chaucer and then generously shared my time with the Classical Education folks to give a presentation on the contents of this book.

Due to changes in the publishing world, this book has wandered, a bit like Odysseus, before finding its way back home again. Jed Donahue at ISI Books saw the value of this project, believed in it, and edited a great deal of the manuscript. I want to thank Tom Spence for his support as the book sailed from one publisher to another. Here at the end, I am very happy that it has at last landed back at its home *oikos* of ISI Books in the hands of Hannah Rowan, who carefully, judiciously, and thoughtfully has brought it to completion.

This book is for Gabe and Ben, who endured too many times when I should have been having fun with them but was instead grading papers, the never-ending work of the English professor. I would also like to dedicate this book in memoriam to John Alvis, who died far too early, in December 2019, robbing the University of Dallas of one of its greatest voices of intellect, wisdom, prudence, and vision. No one was a greater advocate for liberal learning, probing questions, clear arguments, and the permanent things. He started me on this path with one sentence at the bottom of my freshman research paper: "You are ready to begin writing English prose."

INTRODUCTION

To the Student

(Don't skip this. When I was a student, I never bothered with the introductions to books. "Just let me get to the meat of the matter," I thought. Later, I realized that the introduction is where the writer tells you what he's doing and lays out how he's going to do it; he gives you a map for his entire book, allowing you to know where you are going. So read this one, and you will see what I hope you will get out of this book; it will even start you on that process.)

This is a book that can help you write more clearly, more directly, more powerfully, in any field you are studying.

Most of the writing you do in high school and college is persuasive writing—and in fact, most of the writing you will do the rest of your life is persuasive writing. We move from history papers trying to persuade others why and how the French Revolution happened to business proposals about how your company should invest in new marketing strategies or save money through refined supply-chain techniques. And as you probably know, this field has been known since ancient Greece as *rhetoric*—the art of persuading others. What we are doing is making arguments. In the study of rhetoric, the word *argument* does not mean shouting matches; it means reasoned, thoughtful, organized ways of leading our readers to agree with us. I remember a student in my early years of teaching who was pleased with her progress in a Composition 101 class; she wrote, "I want my audience to read my paper and *want* to change their minds to agree with me, not because I beat them into it, but because I've presented the evidence so that they realize they should agree with me." That's a student who had seen into the very heart of what rhetoric is all about.

Arguing therefore means taking up a position or making a claim (the ordinary Greek word for this is a *thesis*) and then persuading others of your position. In your previous writing classes, you may have learned a variety of techniques for helping you to write better. You might have encountered techniques like *brainstorming* and *free writing* and *mapping* to help you with what the ancient Greeks and Romans called *invention*, or getting a topic. Your teachers may have given you further strategies for finding a thesis and sharpening it, and then developing the rest of your paper from there. You might, if you were fortunate, have been introduced to the great tradition of classical rhetoric that runs from Aristotle to Cicero and Quintilian, up through the Middle Ages, into the Renaissance, and even into the modern world, training lawyers, senators, Church officials, political thinkers, and more. Abraham Lincoln, the greatest rhetorician we have ever had as president, was deeply schooled in this tradition. This is the tradition that teaches you that there are three kinds of rhetoric (deliberative, judicial, and epideictic), that there are three kinds of appeals (*ethos*, *logos*, and *pathos*), and that there are six parts of a classical oration (the *exordium*, *narratio*, *partitio*, *confirmatio*, *refutatio*, and *peroratio*).[i] All of these, the classical and the modern concepts, can help you with your writing. All of them have their place, and I have used them all.

But in this book I will show you a particular technique from classical rhetoric that is too often neglected. This technique has helped my students in practical and profound ways—and it can help you as well.

i My colleague Dr. Scott Crider has written a brief and inexpensive guide to the classical rhetorical tradition, *The Office of Assertion*. You should buy it and work through it. Even if you know this tradition, it is a wonderfully succinct guide that will refresh your understanding.

As a teacher, I found good ways to help students find a topic and then to come to a clear, interesting thesis. I figured out ways to get them to write more interesting introductions and conclusions. But often it was in the meat of the argument—the body of the paper—where students fell apart. This is the *dispositio* of the argument, in classical terms—or, we would say, the organization. Organizing arguments is difficult for all of us. Which point should I make first? What evidence do I need to support that point? Which point do I make next, and how do I move on to it? My students struggled here. A promising thesis would be lost by the middle of page three, or the points the writer needed to make somehow got buried. Students would make an interesting subpoint but not support it with evidence. I needed to find a way to help them see the structure of their arguments so they didn't feel they had to make it all up on their own every time. And I needed them to see where the evidence went, and what kind of evidence they needed in the different parts of the argument.

Then I stumbled across stasis theory. This oft-overlooked subfield of classical rhetoric proved to be exactly what my students needed. Stasis theory shows you that there are four basic kinds of arguments. Once I reshaped my composition classes to focus on the Four Arguments, my students' papers became radically more clear, organized, and persuasive.

This approach will help you, too.[ii]

---

ii You can find some other books that teach stasis theory, and I want to acknowledge them here: *Everything's an Argument* by Andrea A. Lunsford, John J. Ruszkiewiecz, and Keith Walters; John D. Ramage, John C. Bean, and June Johnson's *Writing Arguments*; and the now out-of-print *A Rhetoric of Argument* by Jeanne Fahnestock and Marie Secor. These books helped me figure out how to teach this way of understanding argument, and I owe a great deal to all of them. But they are large composition textbooks, with far too much detail for the beginning student. So you end up paying too much money for far too much book. I wanted to create a slim, direct, to-the-point book you would actually use, whose every chapter would have immediate benefits for improving your writing.

What Is Stasis Theory, and How Does It Work?

Stasis theory is a development, or refinement, of rhetorical theories of people like Aristotle and the sophists from ancient Greece. It apparently began with someone named Hermagoras in the second century B.C. Even though we don't have any of his writing, other ancient writers consistently refer to him as having started this theory. Cicero took up stasis theory in his writings, as did Quintilian, but it was Hermogenes, in the second century A.D., who built it into a full system and popularized it.

So what is stasis theory? Like all ancient rhetoric, it is about how arguing happens in the law courts, and it attempts to teach lawyers how to win their cases. Nothing productive can happen in a legal case, the theory says, until the two sides agree about what they are disagreeing about. If one side says, "He stole my cow!" and the other side says, "That is my land," nothing productive can happen; the two sides are arguing completely different issues. So for any argument to be productive (not just in court, but anywhere), we first need to figure out where we have reached *stasis*—that is, where we have reached a stopping point, the point of contention, where we cannot go any further until we have resolved the issue. We often jump ahead to more complex points when we've overlooked the real point of contention—who has the right to have *that* cow on *this* land?

The genius of stasis theory was to discover that we tend to follow a *sequence* in arguing about things, so we can work through a method to discover where we disagree.

Let's imagine that we come upon a scene in the parking lot of a downtown bar. (We will come back to this example throughout this book.) One man is lying on the ground, bleeding profusely from his nose, while the other stands above him, blood on his knuckles. A policeman appears, steps in, and separates the two. Stasis theory teaches us a way to work through this incident in sequence, discovering where the disputes are—what we agree on, and where we need to stop and argue something through.

The sequence looks like this:

Facts. We first need to settle the facts of a case. Who are these two men? Who hit whom? When? How much damage has been sustained on the nose? What was their relationship before the fight?

Definition. If there is no dispute about the facts, we move on to definitions. How do we categorize what happened here? Was it simple assault? Assault with a deadly weapon? Was it perhaps self-defense? The answers matter, for the policeman needs to know whom to arrest. If we cannot agree, we have reached stasis: We will have to argue (if not now, then later, in court) these questions of definition.

Causes (and Effects). The next thing we move to is causes and effects. What actually led to this fight? How did these two men, on an otherwise normal Friday night, end up this way? Did one insult the other? Did one attempt to seduce the other's wife? Did the guy with the bloody nose actually start it by assaulting a third party, and the puncher came to the rescue? And effects: Does the injured man now have a broken nose, and will he need extensive medical attention? (That might factor into a civil case for damages.) You can see that in this case we will probably reach stasis about causes and effects, needing to stop and argue through these questions.

Evaluation. Next, the theory says, we argue about evaluations. Now, we might not see much to dispute here; is anyone going to argue that it was a good thing to punch out another guy on a

Friday night? Well, yes, perhaps they will—if, again, the causal argument showed that the puncher was defending a helpless child or a woman the punchee had been attempting to assault. So we could indeed reach stasis—and need to argue—about whether the assault was a good thing or not.

Policy. At the end of things, we will have to decide what to do about all this, and this could be the place for real argument. Do we convict the puncher? If so, what sentence do we assign? Or do we acquit him and laud him for standing up for the weak and oppressed?

Stasis theory was the first to say that this process—from definition, to causes, to evaluation, to policy—moves in a linear fashion, which clarifies the issue at hand. There is no use deciding the puncher's punishment if we later go back and define his action as self-defense. And there is no point in evaluating what he did as right or wrong if there remains a question over how the altercation came about.

In stasis theory, each of the major issues above centers on a particular question. For definition, it is *"What is this thing?"* For causal arguments, it is *"What caused it or what effects did it have?"* For evaluation, it is *"Is it good or bad?"* And for policy arguments, it is *"What should be done about it?"* By asking these questions, we can discover the point of stasis, because we find that different people have different answers.

This approach works for disputes outside the courts too. Stasis theory helps us understand why people are so divided on certain political and social issues. Take climate change, for instance. One side says, we know exactly what this is (definitional); we know what causes it (causal); we know it is so bad that very soon it could have disastrous effects on our economy, our civilization, our very lives (evaluative); and so we must make massive shifts right now to stave off these terrible consequences (policy). The other side says, I don't even know what this is, and you keep changing the name of it from global warming to climate change to whatever (definitional). Furthermore, I am not sold on the idea that human activity accounts for more than a tiny percentage of the effects you claim to see (causal). Some of your own research suggests that your estimation of the effects is wildly overblown, which leads me to think you are overselling the potentially bad effects of all this (evaluative). So I am not about to vote for any of the massive, trillion-dollar programs you are proposing (policy).

Can you see why we have so much difficulty even talking about this issue in productive ways? One side says, "There's no real dispute about any of this among intelligent people, so let's blow through all the preliminary discussions and get to the policy arguments—not about whether we're going to do anything but how much we are going to do and how quickly." Meanwhile, the other side says, "Hold on a minute—I do not even agree with your facts or your definitions." When neither side agrees on where the stasis is, there is no way to have a productive argument.

The same problem recurs in so many of our political and cultural disputes: The arguments from either side are all over the place, and the different sides do not even agree on what the real issue is. So they end up talking past one another, getting more angry, thinking that the other side is too stupid or too stubborn to understand. Or worse—that the other side is evil for holding their supposedly harmful views. But if they could ever agree on what the issue is, they might come to some productive discussion over the evidence. Stasis theory, then, might be a way to work our way back from a polarized political culture into one in which citizens discuss, debate, and decide in a more thoughtful, generous fashion.

Stasis Theory and Your Writing

So how can stasis theory help you with your own writing—with that history paper that is due in two weeks, or that lab write-up, or that psychology exam that will have an essay portion? Well, in my experience, even students who get a good thesis often have trouble seeing what the real issue is. They get all tangled up in what they are really arguing about, not seeing clearly what questions they are answering. And most important, they often struggle to see that *each of these different kinds of arguments has its own organizational shape.*

To say it a different way, for each of the four kinds of arguments, you need to do different things—in their own order—to persuade others of your point. You do not argue a definitional argument the way you argue a causal argument, and neither of those is quite like an evaluative argument. In this book, I am going to teach you that you must accomplish certain *tasks* for each kind of argument, and you must accomplish them in a certain order. If you can learn how to do this—and you will, as you work through each chapter—you will never again struggle to make clear, organized, and forceful arguments.

This book will teach you how to recognize the four kinds of arguments, how to work through an issue to find where the point of contention is, and then how to organize your own arguments as a clear series of tasks that you need to accomplish as you take the reader through your points. As you master these techniques, your ability to read and critically evaluate others' arguments will soar, too.

Why Mastering These Arguments Is Better Than Using AI

When I first began teaching the Four Arguments, the internet was not exactly new. Long before AI, there was already the threat of students "borrowing" others' words from Wikipedia or wherever and presenting them as their own. We called this, quite correctly, plagiarism. Now, since the explosion of AI tools such as ChatGPT, this is easier than ever: You can ask an AI bot to "give me a definitional argument about *x*" and it will snap one out. In fact, Google, Microsoft, and other services are spending billions in advertising (including during the Super Bowl) to persuade students that they *should* do this. So why not use AI? Doesn't it make it easier for you to get your writing done and move on to other things?

Maybe, but is it worth it? My colleague Deborah Romanick Baldwin talks about it this way with her students: If you pay for a gym membership and then send someone else to the gym to lift for you, you aren't going to get in shape. And if you are trying to learn how to make good arguments and analyze those of others, you aren't going to learn anything from asking AI do that work for you. In fact, you might end up in worse shape: Studies are already showing that those who use AI, especially students, are weakening their "brain muscles." I noticed a similar trend in the early days of Google Maps. People used to navigate even complicated major metropolitan areas simply by looking at a map, finding where they were going, remembering a few landmarks ("turn at the second McDonald's"), and cementing their route in their minds. Today, many people have no idea how to get around unless Captain Google guides them every step of the way. Technology is great, but it can make you stupid if you allow it to. Don't let it keep you from learning what I will present in this book.

So what *are* you learning here? By mastering these four arguments, you are learning how good, clear thinking works. Clear writing is clear thinking, and vice versa. When a student says to me something like "I know what I mean, but I can't seem to write it," I usually respond that no, he doesn't quite know what he means, but working through the writing of his paper will help him to find out what he means. (This is the main reason why schools have for hundreds of years assigned essays and papers as a fundamental assignment in all sorts of subjects.)

Mastering the Four Arguments allows you to *think* them—in conversations with others, in business presentations, and more. If you learn this material by practicing the arguments, as we will in this book, you will be able to make a winning argument on the fly and understand how to respond to counterarguments effectively. And let's be honest: Even in the modern world, we want people to do their own thinking, not rely on some software to do it for them. When your lawyer is presenting your case in court, you don't want her to pull out her phone and ask an AI bot what to say next; you are paying her to know how to analyze the case, remember the precedents, think on her feet, and respond to the judge or other side's lawyers quickly and persuasively.

Do yourself a favor: Go to the rhetorical gym with this book. Do the exercises yourself. Pump some mental iron. Very soon, you'll see your mental muscles grow, your thinking become more clear, and your ability to analyze and answer others' arguments explode.

What Kind of Argument Am I?

One idea I communicate to my students on the first day of class is "You already know how to do this." Arguments are all around you—arguments about politics, the economy, sports, music, the visual arts, you name it. My sons love to argue about the various *Star Wars* films, and sports radio thrives on arguments about which player is the Greatest of All Time, what a certain team should or should not be doing, and which strategies or tactics are the best for the upcoming game. You argue all the time too; you try to convince people of your views on an almost daily basis. You could not have gotten to the point in life where you are holding this book if you were clueless about presenting a position to someone else. *I just want to help you do it better, more precisely, more thoughtfully.*

The first task in using stasis theory is to begin to recognize which of the four kinds of arguments you are dealing with. Let's get started on that.

As I noted above, each of the Four Arguments answers a different question:

- Definitional arguments answer the question “What is this thing?” or perhaps “What kind of thing is this?”
- Causal arguments answer the question “What caused this?” or “What effects did this have?”
- Evaluative arguments answer the question “Is it good or bad (or somewhere in between)?”
- Policy (or problem/solution) arguments answer the question “What should be done about it?”

Below is a set of thesis statements. (Remember, *thesis* is just an ordinary Greek word meaning “the fundamental argument someone is making” or “a claim about reality.”) Read each one carefully and see whether you can determine which of the four kinds of arguments it is making. If you are not sure, ask yourself: *Which of the four questions is this asking?* Try it on your own, and then work through your answers with a partner or a group. The answers are in the footnote, but try to figure them out yourself before looking there.

1. The increase in teen suicide is the result of the decline in basic values in America today.
2. Despite his enormous popularity, Tom Cruise is not a very good actor.
3. Roman Catholics are not really Christians.
4. Though he is little known to Americans today, John Quincy Adams was an effective president who led his country well in difficult times.
5. $e = mc^2$
6. The situation of medical insurance is broken, but rather than go to a single-payer system, we should throw it open to more free competition, as is the case with life insurance.

7. The Beatles are the greatest rock and roll band of all time because of the way they changed both the music and the business of popular music.
8. Pope John Paul II was the most important pontiff of the modern era.
9. Taylor Swift's music has its roots in American blues much more than people realize.
10. Because the laws against marijuana use do more harm than good, we should decriminalize its use on a national level.[iii]

In my experience, students find some of these tricky at first, but once they know the four questions, they are surprised by how easily they can identify the different arguments. The same goes for most of what I will be teaching you. *You already know how to do this.* This is not rocket science. You can master the material in this book with a bit of practice and application, and improve your writing dramatically in a relatively short time.

---

iii I hope you do not look at this footnote until you try the exercise yourself, but once you have tried, feel free to check your work here. #1 is a causal argument; the student is arguing what caused the rise in teen suicide. #2 is an evaluative argument; we are arguing about whether Tom Cruise's acting is good or bad. #3 is a definitional argument; we are saying what Roman Catholics are (or are not). #4 is another evaluative argument; we are arguing over whether Adams was a good or bad president. I like #5 a lot, as it sneaks up on you; it is a definitional argument, saying what energy is. #6 is a policy or problem/solution argument; it argues for what we should do about the broken medical insurance program. #7 might look at first like a causal argument, since in the subordinate clause it talks about the effects the band brought about. But in the main clause, it is an evaluative argument; the subordinate clause just supports the main argument that the Beatles are a great band. Similarly, #8 is an evaluative argument, saying whether John Paul II was good or bad. #9 sometimes trips people up, but notice it is a causal argument; it argues where Swift's music comes from, what caused it to be the way it is. And #10 is a policy or problem/solution argument that starts with a preliminary causal assertion. Just as a disclaimer, these theses do not necessarily convey my own beliefs. Some of them come from student papers, and others from things people have argued with me. For instance, growing up Roman Catholic in the strongly evangelical South, I had classmates argue #3 to my face several times. Many students may not even think of #5 as an argument, but if you think about it for just a moment, you will realize that at some point, Albert Einstein needed to publish a paper *arguing* that this was true. No one before 1905 ever thought this; he *persuaded* physicists that it is so.

Different Arguments, Different Shapes, Different Tasks

Most of us were taught one "shape" or organization for our papers: introduction, body, conclusion. That's not wrong, but it doesn't help you much when you are trying to get your thoughts in order, figuring out what points to make first, second, third, and fourth.

Stasis theory teaches us that each of the Four Arguments takes shape in its own way. A definitional argument has two parts. Causal arguments have a variety of different shapes and orders, and knowing which one to work with is more than half of the battle. Both evaluative arguments and policy arguments have two parts, but in each case, the second part is divided into subparts. In this book, I will teach you the templates that allow you to shape each kind of argument. Once you learn these templates, you will be able to organize your thoughts and know what kind of evidence you need to succeed with each of the different arguments. You will never again be caught in the quandary of not knowing "where this paper is going" in the middle of writing it. You will know which steps or tasks each argument demands of you, and in what order you have to accomplish them, to persuade someone of that kind of argument.

And here is the last, but perhaps the most wide-ranging, effect of mastering stasis theory: Once you know how arguments are supposed to work, you will have a template for critically examining *others'* arguments. You will know a good or bad argument when you see one, and you will know why. You will be able to say, "That's not a very good evaluative argument, because he never established his criteria," or "I agree with her that this is a problem, but she never showed how her solution is better, cheaper, or more feasible than other solutions." You will be able to establish whether a writer is leading you to the truth, whether what he is proposing is good—because you will know how to do this yourself. And that is the whole point of rhetoric—to teach people to distinguish the truth from all the other ideas floating around out there, and to lead others to embrace what is true and follow what is good. That's not a bad goal for a little book on writing, is it?

I want this book to be short, practical, and to the point. So that's enough introduction. The meat of this book is in the next four chapters, where I take you through the Four Arguments of stasis theory, show you how to build each of them, and help you master the tasks needed to be successful with each. Then, in the final chapter, I show how mastering these four arguments in isolation—sort of like learning your scales and arpeggios on an instrument—will help you deal with the more complex, fluid arguments you are likely to make out in the real world. But to get there you must practice the tasks in the first four chapters. This is a book for you to *do*, not just read. I'll ask you to practice each of the steps, learn the templates, and build your own arguments.

Let's get started.

INTRODUCTION
To the Teacher

Where This Book Came From

When I read a book, I often get curious about how the author came to this subject. What made him interested in this topic, and how did he develop this particular argument? I hope that by sharing my story I can help you understand where I am coming from and what I think you can accomplish with this book.

I teach writing. It's what I do. In graduate school I thought I was going to be a scholar of literature, but when I began teaching classes as a lowly T.A., I realized that the real work of being an English professor is to teach writing—to help students get their ideas onto the page in a clear, effective manner. Don't get me wrong; I still love leading students through a discussion of the delicate moral questions of *Sir Gawain and the Green Knight* or the post-postmodern meta-literary questions of *The Canterbury Tales* in my literature courses. But the real investment in time and energy goes into their writing: getting students to articulate a thesis about the literature; clarifying their thinking about subtle uses of diction, figure, and image; and conveying that thinking persuasively to others.

Early in my career, I developed a useful bag of tricks for invention—helping the students brainstorm, map, and otherwise find their way to a topic. I also invented four tests for them to check whether their thesis was a good one (see Appendix 2). I thought that if I could get them as far as the fourth test—seeing an implicit outline in their thesis—the rest would be easy, right? Unfortunately, I found it wasn't so. Students still struggled to organize their points, to follow where the argument was going; they would loop back to previous points, skip steps in their argument, or jump to a completely different argument. Evidence could also be helter-skelter; some of it was good, but in other places it was not germane to the point or was the wrong *kind* of evidence for the argument the student was making.

Somehow, the students were not seeing the shape of their own arguments, or the steps they needed to take to persuade others of their arguments. Simply showing them their thesis and saying, "Do you see the implicit outline here?" or even charting it out with them was not working. I realized that they just didn't seem to understand *how arguments work.*

So I began to look through composition texts that focused on argumentation and found three that were well known and helpful: Lunsford, Ruszkiewicz, and Walters's *Everything's an Argument*; Fahnestock and Secor's *Rhetoric of Argument*; and John D. Ramage, John C. Bean, and June Johnson's *Writing Arguments.* These showed me that there are only four kinds of argument—or five at most—and more importantly, that each of these has a different outline, or shape. "Great," I thought. "This is what I need." But each of these books is huge and expensive. Each covers far more material than just these four arguments, with sections on research skills, style, etc., etc.—things I could teach myself. Each includes sample essays on subjects that are dated by the time the book is published (making a new edition necessary every few years). And each tends, in its sample arguments and essays, to lean pretty predictably to the moderate-left side of the political spectrum, a bias I find dreary and students even at state institutions where I've taught think monotonous and uninspiring.

What I need, I thought, is a simple, stripped-down version of those books, focusing on just the Four Arguments, explaining where they come from, why they are important, and how they work. A book on writing should be slim, practical, concise—and relatively inexpensive. That is what I have produced in this book—both for you and your students.

So What Is Stasis Theory?

Some of you may already be familiar with the classical tradition of rhetoric that begins with the sophists teaching in ancient Greece, gets its best orderly consideration in Aristotle, and flowers throughout the rest of the ancient period through thinkers such as Cicero and Quintilian. Stasis theory is a part of that tradition; it was immensely popular through the Renaissance and Early Modern period, but is not so well known today. The books referenced above are some of the few that keep it alive; standard histories of Western rhetoric give it a passing reference but do not really acknowledge stasis theory's important influence, so that many who teach writing by means of classical rhetoric today know the parts of a "Ciceronian" oration and the categories by which to discover a topic in his *De Inventione* but may have never heard of stasis theory or know how it can help. In fact, I find that rhetoric and composition teachers who learned from Lunsford, Ruszkiewicz, and Walters, or Fahnestock and Precor, and who might not care much about classical rhetoric, know more about stasis theory (even if they do not call it by that name) than those deeply imbedded in the "classical education" movement, where the classical rhetorical tradition is taught with more frequency.

As I note in the introduction to students, stasis theory, like all rhetorical teaching, began in the law courts as a way to clarify the nature of legal disputes. It is a way of deciding where the legal issue really lies. The two sides might agree upon certain facts but might disagree sharply about other issues. Stasis theory gives an order to working through these questions: from facts, to definitions, to causes, to evaluations, and finally to policy. Stasis theory says that when the two sides find their point of conflict, they have reached *stasis*—the point at which they must stop and argue, rationally presenting their views. There is no point in going on to more complex issues while the point of stasis is at this more fundamental stage.

Each stage also has a fundamental question attached to it that sharpens the mind and helps one find the point of stasis. Take for example a car accident, a simple fender bender. The facts may not be in dispute: Two cars have damaged front fenders and bumpers. Definitions may not be in dispute: Everyone knows what an automobile accident is. (But maybe not: Was this an intentional act or an unintentional one? Was it a hit-and-run? But let's keep it simple and say that this accident was clearly accidental and both parties are present.) The next stage is causal: How did this happen, and what effects does it have? Who caused the two cars to collide? How much damage is there? Now we might have the proper place for the dispute. After that, we move on to evaluation: Is this a good thing or a bad thing? Well, clearly it's not good, so there is no point of stasis to argue about here. Finally, we reach the policy stage: What should be done about this? And here we again might have a real dispute: Who is going to pay for the repairs, and how much? Will that take us back to the causal arguments and a finding that both sides are partially responsible and thus each will assume a percentage of the cost? Or will it find one side exclusively responsible and place the financial burden on him?

You can see how stasis theory gives us clarity on the right questions to ask, the right arguments to have, and tells us that there is no use arguing about a later stage ("Who is going to pay for this?") until we have decided a more fundamental question ("How did this happen? Who caused it to happen?"). It also shows us where we might otherwise waste our time arguing about inconsequential matters—although I admit I can imagine two philosophers at the scene of a fender bender, scratching their heads and asking one another, "Well, really we must begin with 'What, after all, is an automobile?'" "Is an automobile with a crumpled-in fender still a 'good' automobile, or does it lack integrity, clarity, and resonance?" "Was banging into my colleague's car in the campus parking lot an unethical act or merely an unpropitious happenstance?"

I know I'm being a bit silly here, but I hope you see the point: Stasis theory will allow your students to get from a general topic to the precise question they need to ask in order to find the kind of argument they really want to make. From there, they will be able to organize their thoughts much more rapidly and effectively.

Why This Book Is Useful

I set aside teaching the Four Arguments for some time while teaching literature in our Core Curriculum here at the University of Dallas. At first, I thought these four types did not fit what I was doing in those classes. (I'll come back to that assumption in chapter 5, and show how I was wrong.) But in the meantime, I had begun to read about the historical background of the Four Arguments and discovered the underappreciated classical rhetorical field of stasis theory that underlies the work of Lunsford, Ruszkiewicz, and Walters; Fahnestock and Secor; and Ramage, Bean, and Johnson. I share some of that history in the introduction to students above, but what I want to emphasize here is just how practical and useful I have found the framework of stasis theory in my own classes. Students comment that it has taken so much of the mystery out of crafting arguments and made writing papers seem like common sense.

The great thing about stasis theory is that it takes the writer all the way through the writing process, from invention through revision. By showing students that there is a sequence to examining the unfocused, still-nascent questions in their mind, stasis theory helps them quickly discover the real issue they want to investigate. For example, take climate change (a hot-button issue common in other argumentation books): Students can be overwhelmed by how much there is to say. But by taking them through stasis theory's sequence of questions, they can begin to see where they want to enter the discussion and find what they have to argue about it. So, for instance, do they want to argue what climate change is, what its qualities are? Do they want to argue, instead, what causes climate change and what its effects are? Do they want to make an argument for how bad it is, or how it is not nearly as bad as others are making it out to be? Do they want to articulate proposals for what to do about it? Unlike brainstorming, clustering, or mapping—all of the invention techniques taught in most composition textbooks, which generate topics but still leave the student groping for how to organize the material and identify the central question, stasis theory shows that there is an order to the questions people ask about an issue, and that these questions build upon one another.

Once students see which question they are really asking, stasis theory makes it easy for them to organize the essay that will result from asking that question. You will see this yourself as you work the students through the chapters. After they grasp the structure of each kind of argument and internalize its template, they can move quickly from invention to organization, crafting a clear outline—or, as I will call it throughout this book, a set of tasks to accomplish—for the rest of the paper. And this set of tasks will help them to identify the kind of evidence each different argument will require in order for them to be persuasive.

When students learn stasis theory and the structure of each of the Four Arguments, their ability to engage with others' arguments soars. After they understand that an evaluative argument must set up criteria and show that the subject at hand (a cello performance, a film, a dish of ratatouille) must meet those criteria—that these are the tasks all successful evaluative arguments must complete—then they have in their heads a set of critical tools for examining all of the arguments around them every day. They see a causal argument and notice that the writer confused necessary and sufficient causes; they see a definitional argument and recognize the writer did not define the predicate precisely; they see a policy argument (or, as I will call it, a problem/solution argument) and point out that the writer did not show how her solution is at all feasible. These rubrics will, by the end of this book, be second nature to the students, and they will read others' arguments with more facility, intelligence, and proper skepticism.

How to Use This Book

This is not a book for reading in the easy chair next to the fireplace. You and your students will want to work through the exercises in each chapter so they can internalize the structures and procedures of stasis theory. Students should produce topics for invention, outlines, drafts, and even revised papers as you work through the book with them. (Not every outline, of course, must lead to a draft, nor every draft to a revision, nor every revision to a final, edited paper. Often thinking of this process as a pyramid—with lots of practice in the early stages leading to a few final products—is the best pedagogical method. And it reflects what professional writers do: I don't know about you, but I have many pieces of writing in each of these stages.) Most of the book is not rocket science; I'm sure you are a wonderful, dedicated teacher and will find your own ways to engage the students with this material. But if you'd like some help, or just a new idea or two, I have included in the endnotes some suggestions based on what has worked in my classes. (I have addressed the footnotes largely to the students, but you might enjoy them too. If the more industrious students find their way to the endnotes, well, we'll just have to give them a peek behind the curtain, won't we? I saw no reason to make you buy a separate teacher's edition just for those simple suggestions.)

The book has only five chapters, and only a few exercises in each chapter, but these exercises are crucial. Have your students read the material of the chapter, and discuss with them some of the issues that the chapter brings up. For instance, in chapter 1, it is instructive to pause and have the students try to define "athlete." They all know what one is—or think they do—but providing a precise stipulative definition is much trickier than they might realize, and it impresses upon them how much intellectual effort is needed to craft a good definition. But you can also allow these exercises to open up into wider discussions about the issues themselves if you like. I give gentle prompts for these kinds of discussions throughout the book.

I also give a short excursus on some larger implications of the material in each chapter, providing a wider philosophical context for the given argument to provoke students to that liberal education that leads them out of opinion into the truths of things. You may do with these sections as you will. I hope they can lead to genuine liberal learning experiences, but if they are not your cup of tea, you can safely ignore them. You won't hurt *my* feelings.

I know that some teachers who are committed to a certain kind of "classical" or "liberal" education want students to exercise all of their mental effort on elevated topics and texts, and I see the good in that. I teach in the strongly Great Books–focused Core Curriculum at the University of Dallas, and I know well the good it produces for students. But sometimes it helps, when learning a new art, to lower the bar slightly at first. When students are brainstorming for topics, it often helps to start with their own interests, hobbies, and activities. Those are the places where they already know the arguments swirling around them, and where they might already have partially formed arguments in their heads. Many semesters, I start my first course by asking students, "In what field are you an expert?" Now, many college students do not believe they are an expert in anything, so I lower the bar. I ask them, "What activity or hobby have you been doing for a number of years? Is it playing the trumpet in band? Dance? Wood carving?" If you have one of these, I say, you know much more about that activity than the general population does; that's all I mean by being an expert. And therefore, I say, "You probably have opinions, ideas, about how to do it well and how it is done poorly; you know problems, issues, and controversies in that field. Start there." I would rather have students who are learning about arguments write—at least at the beginning—from a position of knowledge than from complete ignorance. I'd rather have a great paper about the real problems in Irish dance competitions than an airy, clueless paper about justice in Plato's *Symposium*, which the student read hurriedly and on which the student, at this point, has no considered opinions, no real stake.

But I do think that students *should* engage with the complex arguments that great texts present, so at the end of each of the four main chapters in this book I have included an argument from a classical text. These are indeed challenging for students. They are challenging for me. But by wrestling with what Hamlet is arguing in "To be or not to be" or how Portia defines mercy in her "Quality of Mercy" speech, students can really stretch their reading and analytical abilities about how arguments work.

Finally, in the introduction to students, I addressed an issue that wasn't even on the horizon when I started drafting this book, but is now everywhere—AI and especially students' use of it—and I'll add just a few words here. I don't think I am saying anything remarkable by observing that the period we are going through is many times more revolutionary than the Gutenberg revolution, a period I know well as a late-medieval scholar. It took nearly two hundred years before people fully understood the changes the printing press had made—in everything—and I suspect that those of us living in the midst of the digital revolution have few resources, and little perspective, to come to terms with what is happening in a comprehensive way. But in the two years since AI has gone mainstream, we have already seen a change in attitudes about ChatGPT and similar software applications. People are exploring its uses as a tool but also discovering its troubling potential to affect users' capacity for real, independent thought. In my view, AI will create a new revolution in the need for the *truly* liberal arts; it will make it even more obvious that what humans need, and what we do best, when we are at the top of our mental game, is "right-brain," creative, higher-order liberating thinking, not the mechanical putting together of mere repetitive patterns. And that means we need good arguments, made by humans who can understand context, environment, history, philosophical implications, and theological meaning.

If you have questions, want to share with me your teaching triumphs with the book, or criticize its inevitable shortcomings so I can improve it for a later edition, don't hesitate to write. I'd love to hear from you. My address is roper@udallas.edu.

CHAPTER ONE

DEFINITIONAL ARGUMENTS

What is this thing?

We begin our work with the Four Arguments of stasis theory by looking at the most fundamental type of argument, *definition.* A definitional argument answers the question "What is this thing?" We are trying to determine into what category something fits. Is a tomato a vegetable or a fruit? Is that car an SUV or something else? These are definitional arguments.

You might look at the title of this chapter, or at those two examples above, and think, "Definitions? People don't *argue* about definitions, do they? Definitions are not things you dispute about; you just look up the word in the dictionary, you see what it means, it's all decided." You can look up whether a tomato is a fruit or not. (Hint: It is.) You can look up whether Honda calls that vehicle an SUV or a truck or something else. There's no argument when it comes to definitions. Right?

Don't you believe it.

People argue about definitions all the time. These arguments take on enormous significance. You might hear someone say, "Access to health care is a universal right." Okay, you might respond, but how are you defining *health care*? What do you mean by *access*? How do you define the word *right*? If two people discussing the topic define those terms differently, they will struggle to have a fruitful discussion, much less come to any agreement.

Let's think back to our scene outside the bar. A man is lying in the parking lot of a downtown bar, blood spurting from his nose. Another guy stands above him with blood on his knuckles. Remember, in stasis theory we first establish the facts. But the facts might not, and probably do not, solve anything on their own. What do you call this collection of facts? With what term do you define it and thus give it meaning?

Does that sound confusing or abstract? Okay, let's try to be more concrete: *The police arrest the puncher. What do they charge him with?* Is it simple misdemeanor assault? Assault and battery? Felonious assault? What happens when the man (or later, his lawyer) calls this event an act of self-defense? *The answer matters,* in all sorts of ways. The definition is important. It will determine what class of crime the district attorney charges the puncher with and thus the punishment meted out if the puncher is convicted. It will determine how the prosecution and defense will pursue their legal strategies, and what evidence they will present.[1]

Definitions, and arguments about them, extend well beyond the courtroom. I happened to be reading the *Atlanta Journal-Constitution* one day in 1999 and saw an article with the title "Hollow Cheers."[i] The article presented a fascinating argument over the question, what is a cheerleader? More specifically, is a cheerleader an athlete? This is not an abstract question.[2] To help you see why, let me pose a different question: Which side do you think the football coaches in Georgia took on this question? You might think they would have argued a firm no, that cheerleaders cannot be athletes the way our tough, strong football players are. But you would be wrong, and the reason why can be given in two simple words: Title IX. You see, according to that federal statute, schools must offer proportional athletic opportunities for men and women based on

i Mike Fish, with assistance from David A. Milliron, "Hollow Cheers," *Atlanta Journal-Constitution*, December 18, 1999. Used by permission.

the percentages of each gender in the overall school population. So if a school's student body is 53 percent women, it must have a proportional offering of athletic programs for women. Now perhaps you can see why this definition is significant. If the schools called cheerleaders (the great majority of whom are female) "athletes," they could solve their Title IX problems without reducing football rosters or cutting other men's sports.[3]

So definitions matter. Deciding what something is, or is not, leads to crucial decisions in business, politics, law, medicine, education, and more. You will often find a definition at the core of the argument over hot-button topics.[4] For example:

- Is assisted suicide a crime?
- What is a marriage? Is it "the union of one man and one woman," or do you accept a broader definition of marriage that would allow gay couples to be married? The U.S. Supreme Court ruled for a broader definition. Would you include polyamory—three or more partners—in your definition of marriage?
- What is the status of a child inside its mother's womb? Is it a "child," a "fetus," a "collection of cells"? Is it the possession of the mother, or does it have its own individual status?
- How do you define sexual assault—or to say it a different way, what gets included in the category "sexual assault," and what do we exclude?
- Is marijuana a "gateway drug," often leading to abuse of much more dangerous drugs? Or is it a relatively harmless recreational drug that therefore should be legal across the United States? Are there other options beyond this either/or dichotomy?

Learning how to argue well about definitions, and how to evaluate critically others' definitional arguments, is a crucial skill in becoming a thoughtful citizen—and even more, in becoming liberally educated, in freeing yourself from biases so you can understand and follow the truth.

The Language and Types of Definition

As we pursue the Four Arguments, it will help to learn the vocabulary and concepts of each type. This allows us to be more precise in our language, and often helps in practical ways, by giving us a sense of the best definition to use in a given situation. Though you have used definitions your entire life, you may not have studied them formally or know the vocabulary. So let's take a quick look at the different kinds of definitions.[ii]

By example. The least formal type of definition is the definition by example. You define by example when you point to a kind of thing as a way of illustrating what you are talking about. When you say something like "Classic rock is, you know, like the Rolling Stones or Led Zeppelin," or "A university is a place like Yale," or "Rap is the music that Snoop Dogg and Eminem make," you are defining by example. In this kind of definition, you don't lay out the specifics of your subject. You hope that by pointing to an example, your audience will understand the category you are talking about.

Operational. Here you define by telling us what process determines something's nature or type—what happens in the presence of something, or especially what measurable results are produced

ii There are more than these three, and in the Notes for Teachers I mention some books that discuss several other kinds of definitions. But I want to keep this discussion on the practical level for you, and for that, you really only need to be aware of these three.

in this process. "A starch is a substance that turns an iodine stain dark blue": You define a starch not by its qualities alone but also by how you know when you have one or, to say it a different way, what operations let you know something is a starch.

Stipulative. This is the kind of definition we are normally thinking about when we use the term. In a stipulative definition, you set out carefully—or *stipulate*—what something is. You first name the *genus*, or general category of thing to which our item belongs, and then differentiate it carefully from others in that category by showing to what *species* it belongs. So D (definition) = G (genus) + S (species). "A chimpanzee is an ape that..."; "A sonnet is a lyric poem that has fourteen lines and follows a particular rhyme scheme . . ."; "Sexual assault is an encounter wherein..." For a definition like this to work, you must first name the genus well, putting the thing in its correct general category. It does no good to call a sonnet "a kind of novel," for instance; you are already off the mark. Then you must distinguish your item from other, similar things that belong to this genus, so that only your thing, and no others, can fit into what you are talking about. "A chimpanzee is an ape with hair" doesn't distinguish a chimp from other kinds of apes. "A sonnet is a poem that's rather short" doesn't differentiate it from other kinds of short poems. So to have a good stipulative definition, you must get both the genus (the broad category) and the species (the differentiating factor that isolates this one item) right.[5]

How to Create Effective Definitional Arguments

So we have established that a definitional argument answers the question "What is this thing?" or, perhaps more subtly, "What kind of thing is this?" And we have established that we need to make these kinds of arguments all the time. How do we do it well?

Well, let's go back to our example from the *Atlanta Journal-Constitution.* Is a cheerleader an athlete? How would you develop this argument: *"Cheerleaders are athletes"*? Now, remember what I said in the introduction: you already know how to do this. You've been making these kinds of arguments since you were very young. In any definitional argument, *the first thing you must do is define the predicate,* the part *after* the state-of-being verb that functions like an equal sign in an equation:

Cheerleaders are athletes

Right? You first need to define *athlete* and make sure your audience agrees with your definition.

So what's an athlete? How would you define one? How do you create a clear understanding of this term?

You may think it odd to define something in order to define something else. Are you moving down an unending path? Perhaps in the realm of philosophy, but rhetoric is a *practical* pursuit. So let's say it this way: *You must define the predicate in a way that is acceptable to your audience.* You need something that leads your audience to the truth of things. Often you start by drafting a definition and then testing it and refining it until you have something that gets at the truth in a way your audience will accept.

So how about something like this? "An athlete is one who engages in regular strenuous exercise and maintains a high level of fitness and physical ability." That sets up the genus + species pretty well, right? That includes just about everyone I want to include, excludes those I want to exclude, and gets at the essence of what I think an athlete is in a way that just about all of my audience will agree with.

But there may be some wrangling here. A good rhetor anticipates objections from his audience. "But doesn't an athlete have to compete in some way?" you might say. "You're not really an athlete unless you are playing competitive games or running in races or something like that, right?" Well, I'd say no. The woman who runs just for herself, never competes, but can run a 4:30 mile, or a marathon's distance in two and a half hours—you're telling me she's not an athlete? So I want to add this to my definition: "whether he or she competes in official competitions or not." Now I have constructed this definition to grasp what I believe are the essentials. I wanted to include as many of the crucial elements as I could without excluding people as athletes whom I didn't want to exclude.

Okay, now that you have defined the predicate, what do you have to do to complete the persuasive argument? *You need to show that the subject fits in the category of the predicate.* You have to show that cheerleaders have the qualities of, and belong to the group that you just defined as, athletes. And how do you do this? Description and examples provide the crucial kinds of evidence that will "win" this argument for you. You need to show cheerleaders: what they are, what they do, how they spend their time, how they "engage in strenuous physical activity" and "maintain a high level of fitness and physical ability." You can do that by giving examples of what cheerleaders do on a regular basis. *And once you do that, you will have succeeded in your definitional argument*; you will persuade your audience, if they are fair-minded and listen to the case you have built.

So what have we learned? Well, a great deal of practical information about how to organize and prosecute this kind of argument. Let's take a look.

A definitional argument will

- Have two parts:
  - So already you know what the outline will look like. It won't have three body parts, like the old "five-paragraph paper" told you to have—*only two.* (See below for my dislike of the old five-paragraph essay format.) And

you don't need to figure out the content for each of those parts—just by looking at the definitional thesis statement, you can *see* it.

- Accomplish two tasks to be successful:
  - It must define the predicate clearly and convincingly.
  - It must show that the subject fits in the category of the predicate.
- Feature a particular kind of evidence:
  - It will tend to have a healthy number of examples.
  - It will tend to describe the subject and predicate well.

Therefore, as you think about a definitional argument, you should have a template in your head:

I. Define the predicate
II. Show that the subject fits in the category of the predicate

So for your argument about cheerleaders, the structure looks like this:

I. An athlete is one who engages in regular strenuous exercise and maintains a high level of fitness and physical ability, whether he or she competes in official competitions or not.
II. Cheerleaders engage in regular strenuous exercise and maintain a high level of fitness and physical activity; therefore, they are athletes.

In classical rhetorical terms, this is the *dispositio*, or the organization, of your paper's argument. The nice thing is that once you realize you are making a definitional argument, you don't have to flail around trying to figure out how to organize the paper—it's right here for you! Furthermore, you know what kind of evidence you need, and where. In section I above, you will present a broad representation of people who can show what athletes are—and perhaps some counterexamples of people who are not athletes. Then, in section II, you will need to show only that cheerleaders engage in regular strenuous exercise and maintain a high level of fitness, and presto—you have persuaded your audience.

Notice that you need to do these things not because I told you to do it this way, or your teacher says to do this—it's because *those are the tasks you must accomplish, in that order, if you want to be successful in this kind of argument.*[6] And once you see arguing as *a set of tasks to be accomplished,* rather than "weird stuff my teacher makes me do," everything becomes, if not easy, at least clear and straightforward.

Critical Thinking/Reading Skills

This template will not only help you write your own arguments. It will also help you be a better critical reader of others' arguments. Now, as you read someone else's argument and realize it is making a definitional argument, you can hold the writer to these standards: Did she define the predicate adequately? Do you think the writer included everything in the predicate that needs to be included, and excluded the things that need to be excluded? Then, did she show adequately that the subject fits in the category of the predicate? Did the writer provide adequate examples and evidence showing that the subject fits in the category of the predicate? Can you think of things that the writer could have included but left out, or things that she should have excluded but did not?

EXERCISES

Exercise 1.1 Brainstorm some sample definitional arguments. (It often helps to do this with a partner, or three or four people, but if you are alone you can still do this.) You might be inspired by some of the arguments below, ones my students have used. They range from the serious to the silly. Playing around with these arguments may help you generate ideas. (I note here that many of these theses and arguments are controversial; I do not agree with all of them.)[7]

- Ketchup is not a vegetable.[8]
- Alcoholism is a disease, not a condition.[9]
- Someone who supports laissez-faire capitalism is not a conservative.
- Abraham Lincoln was/was not a white supremacist.[10]
- Pie is a breakfast food.[11]
- Beauty is an objective reality, not a subjective perspective of the mind.
- Sex, gender, and social gender traits are different things.[12]
- Ballerinas are artists, not athletes.
- Online friends are not real friends.
- Flip-flops are shoes.[13]
- Leggings are/are not pants.[14]
- Halfpipe snowboarding is a sport.[15]
- Decaffeinated coffee is not real coffee.
- Recess is a school subject, not a waste of time.
- *Die Hard* is a Christmas movie.[16]
- America is less a melting pot than a salad bowl.
- Hong Kong's afternoon tea is not the traditional English tea.
- Single-character plays are not true theater.

- Viruses are not living things.
- Metaphors are implicit fallacies of equivocation.[17]
- Listening silently is active learning.
- The human mind is not a computer.
- Online public education is not homeschooling.

You might notice how many of these arguments are negative definitions—saying that "*x* is not *y*" rather than that "*x* is *y*." Saying what something is *not* can be an important part of establishing what it *is*. Doing so can clear out faulty ideas that you know at least some in your audience have heard and may accept. Then you can make the positive argument more effectively. Take the argument "The human mind is not a computer." With this formulation, you negate the idea that the mind is merely a computer, a logical, programmable, mechanical piece of electronics. You are also suggesting that the mind is something broader, deeper, and more complex than even the most sophisticated machine.

Exercise 1.2 Now take your definitional thesis and map out how you would argue it. If it helps, go back and look at the template for a definitional argument. Here are some questions to consider:

- How would you define the predicate?
- How can you make that predicate include what you want to include and exclude what you want to exclude?
- How can you make sure the predicate is acceptable to your audience? (Can you anticipate objections and answer them?)
- How will you show that the subject fits in the category of the predicate?
- What evidence will you use? What examples will be the best ones to use to be persuasive?

Exercise 1.3 When you are ready, write up your definitional argument. By now it should be quite clear what you are doing, the order in which you are doing it, and how you will put together the paragraphs. You see? Once you understand how these arguments work, what tasks you need to accomplish, and the order in which you need to accomplish these tasks, writing arguments (that is, persuasive essays, thesis-driven papers, whatever you or your teachers and professors choose to call them) is much less mystifying.

Further Reflections: Definitional Arguments, Organization, and the Old "Five-Paragraph Essay"

Someday I hope to have written on my tombstone, "Here lies Gregory Roper, who finally killed off the five-paragraph essay."

You know what I'm talking about, right? It's the basic design of an essay or paper many of us were taught, and it looks like that which is on the opposite page:[iii]

Now, let me say that there is some—a wee bit—of usefulness to learning this form. It teaches young students (I'm thinking middle school) that there must be *some* kind of organization, *some* form, to give an essay coherence. It teaches that there must be an introduction, a body, and a conclusion. All well and good.

But there are many problems. For instance, why do all introductions have to start broadly and end in a narrowing that leads to the thesis? Many excellent published introductions work differently (see Dr. Scott Crider's book *The Office of Assertion* for helpful advice on different kinds of introductions). Similarly, why does a conclusion have to start narrowly and broaden out? Why do we have to recap the three main points? Has your writing been that confusing that the reader will have forgotten your points so quickly? Is the reader that stupid or forgetful?

iii This chart appears on the website AssignmentEssayHelp.com in the article "How to Write an Academic Essay?," by Audrey Brown, posted January 6, 2016. But it can be found in thousands of places all across the internet.

Basic 5-Paragraph Essay Graphic Organizer

I. **Paragraph I**: Introduce Topic

THREE Supportive Ideas (A, B, C)

THESIS STATEMENT

II. **Paragraph II**: Introduce and support your **first** supportive idea with three pieces of evidence.
   a. Topic Sentence
      i. Evidence
      ii. Evidence
      iii. Evidence
   b. Concluding Sentence

III. **Paragraph III**: Introduce and support your **second** supportive idea with three pieces of evidence.
   a. Topic Sentence
      i. Evidence
      ii. Evidence
      iii. Evidence
   b. Concluding Sentence

IV. **Paragraph IV**: Introduce and support your **third** supportive idea with three pieces of evidence.
   a. Topic Sentence
      i. Evidence
      ii. Evidence
      iii. Evidence
   b. Concluding Sentence

V. **Paragraph V:**
Restate Thesis Statement

RECAP three main supportive ideas (A, B, C)

Overall Concluding Statement

Here's my main problem: Why do there always have to be three points? What if you don't have three points? I can distinctly remember writing papers where I had four really good, important, interlocking points. Because I'd been taught this form, I lopped off one of them before finishing the paper. When I got the comments back, the professor wrote something like "You were doing well but then never got to the logical next step, which would have been to argue *x*." And I remember thinking—I can see myself like it was yesterday, standing there holding the paper in my hands, frustrated at the grade—*"Because then it would have had four points—and the five-paragraph essay is supposed to have only three points! That's what Ms. Jones taught me in tenth-grade English!"* Or I had only two points—two really solid points that I thought proved my argument—and so what did I do? I got out the shovel and started piling on the manure for another paragraph so I'd have three points. When I got the paper back—again, I'm not kidding about this—the professor wrote something like "You did a good job and proved your argument in the first two body paragraphs, but then why did you add this third point? It's unnecessary and largely irrelevant." And I remember thinking, *"Because I'm supposed to have three points! Ms. Jones said we always had to have three points!"*

Well, you might say, Signor Roper, you were silly and uninformed—you should have known that the model allows for a variable number of body paragraphs. But the model is rarely taught that way. (And by the way, it is *never* pictured that way—the image always has three, and only three, rectangles for the body paragraphs. "Three shall be the number thou shalt count, and the number of the counting shall be three. Four shalt thou not count, neither count thou two, excepting that thou then proceed to three. Five is right out.")[iv] There

iv If you don't know the reference here—to the instructions from *Armaments*, Chapter Two, for the Holy Hand Grenade of Antioch—it is time you YouTubed one of the funniest scenes in cinema history.

seems to be something magical, something of the numerological, about the number three that has gotten stuck on this model.

And that leads to an even more damaging habit I have seen time and again in students: The model becomes prescriptive, and they simply cannot think of essay topics in anything but lists of three. This is where you get thesis statements like "Flannery O'Connor uses characterization, symbolism, and interesting diction in 'A Good Man Is Hard to Find.'" Why just these three things? Doesn't she use other things as well? And what's the relationship between these three things? Does one build on the other, exist in tension with the other two—what? And to what purpose does she use these things? You see, the five-paragraph essay form leads to essays that are just lists—detachable sets of three concepts or features, with no real connection between them.[v] Unfortunately, students who have had this model drummed into them struggle to think in any other way. And they become deeply invested in this form because they think it *works*—it gives them a reliable structure that, they think, will fit any assignment. I once had a student—an intelligent student, really great in class discussions—who wrote every paper in this stilted, artificial format. When I challenged her to move beyond it, she said, angrily, "That is the way I write. That is the way I was taught to write. That's the only way I can do it, and that's the only way I'm *going* to do it." My heart sank. Here was this fascinating young woman, and her writing wasn't nearly as good as her mind because this clunky, artificial format had become a straitjacket. It took me the rest of the semester to get her to see that her very interesting thoughts died when she tried to force them into the five-paragraph box.

v My friend and colleague Dr. Andrew Moran says it this way: the five-paragraph essay form encourages students to think of the body of the paper *horizontally*—the three points just a list "with no clear causal connections between them"—as opposed to *vertically*, where each point leads to the next, "a clear line of causation linking proof to proof, one proof subordinate to the other so that all have a particular place in the argument." Writers end up with lists, not proofs, and the argument "tends to be superficial."

By now I hope you can see that *definitional arguments don't work in the five-paragraph format.* If you tried to come up with three body paragraphs for "Cheerleaders are really athletes," you would have a complete mismatch with the tasks you need to complete to be persuasive. There are only two tasks here: defining the predicate and showing that the subject fits in the category of the predicate. Do that, in that order, and you'll persuade people of your definitional arguments. Adding a third section would at best be irrelevant, probably confuse your reader, and make you less persuasive. The form your argument takes must fit with the tasks you need to accomplish.

With the next three kinds of arguments, you'll see that each has *its* own form—because the tasks each is trying to accomplish are different. You will begin to see how different arguments work in different ways, and you will broaden the scope of your argumentative excellence.

EXTRA FUN WITH DEFINITIONAL ARGUMENTS

A Classic Definitional Argument[18]

Portia's "Quality of Mercy" Speech from *The Merchant of Venice* (4.1.183–201)

Now that you have begun mastering definitional arguments, why not see whether this skill can help you with a classic text from the great literary tradition? You could try this on Shakespeare's Sonnet 116, which creates first a negative definition of love ("Love is not love / which alters when it alteration finds") and then proceeds to a positive definition of love ("It is an ever-fixed mark"). But I thought I would give you a bit more of a challenge: Portia's wonderful "Quality of Mercy" speech from *The Merchant of Venice.*

Portia disguises herself as a lawyer in a court to help her husband's friend Antonio get out of a sticky situation: he has promised Shylock, a Jew, a pound of his flesh if he could not pay back a rather sizable loan of 3,000 ducats, and since Antonio cannot pay it back, it looks like Antonio will die. Portia urges Shylock to be merciful. Shylock retorts, "On what compulsion must I? Tell me that." He clearly sees no legal reason to offer mercy to Antonio. And in fact Portia offers no legal argument; instead, she offers this argument about why we should be, why we must be, merciful.

As you read the speech, think about the structure of a definitional argument. How does Portia define mercy? Does she define the predicate? Does she show that the subject fits in the category of the predicate? What evidence and examples does she give to suggest that the subject fits in the category of the predicate? How does she expand the definition of mercy from what most of us might think it is?

The quality of mercy is not strained;[vi]
It droppeth as the gentle rain from heaven
Upon the place beneath. It is twice blest;
It blesseth him that gives and him that takes.
'Tis mightiest in the mightiest; it becomes
The thronèd monarch better than his crown.
His scepter shows the force of temporal power,
The attribute to awe and majesty,
Wherein doth sit the dread and fear of kings;
But mercy is above this scept'red sway;
It is enthronèd in the hearts of kings,
It is an attribute to God himself,
And earthly power doth then show likest God's
When mercy seasons justice. Therefore, Jew,
Though justice be thy plea, consider this:
That, in the course of justice, none of us
Should see salvation. We do pray for mercy,
And that same prayer doth teach us all to render
The deeds of mercy.

Discuss with your classmates how well Portia constructs her definitional argument. Perhaps you could write out her "thesis" and then her supporting statements. Now that you have studied definitional arguments, do you think she is successful in creating this argument? Are lines 196–201 even part of her definitional argument, or are they doing something else?

vi Portia in this first line puns on "strained," which can mean "with great effort"—as when we strain to do something. But surely she is also eliding the prefix "con" at the beginning of the word, so she is saying that mercy is not "constrained"; no one is compelled, ever, to be merciful.

CHAPTER TWO

CAUSAL ARGUMENTS

What caused this or what effects did it have?

Stasis theory says that after we have defined a subject, the next question to consider is "What caused it or what effects did it have?" After defining our downtown bar parking lot fight as felonious assault, we will begin investigating how this whole thing happened. What led to that one man lying in the parking lot with a bloody nose? Well, clearly, a fight, and the other man's hand punching him in the face. What caused the fight? An argument. What caused the argument? One man talking to another man's wife. But how did we get from a conversation to a fight? Surely many complex factors were involved. The prosecution and defense will each attempt to set up a kind of narrative, a chain of events, one leading to or causing the other, in order to accuse or exonerate the man who broke the other's nose. And if a civil case arises, where the battered man asks for financial recompense, we might get into the *effects* of the fight: a broken nose, perhaps a concussion, expensive hospital trips, time and income lost from work, damage to the man's reputation and prestige.[1]

You may have been a little skeptical of the idea that we argue about definitions, but I am guessing that you are not skeptical about this kind of argument, because we argue about causes all the time.

- Why won't that door close properly? What is causing it to stick?
- What is causing that funny sound to come from under the hood of my car? (Not long ago I witnessed two mechanics standing in front of my thirteen-year-old Toyota Camry having exactly this argument.)
- What happens when we remove wolves as apex predators from a particular environment?
- How did the Red Sox manage to win the World Series that year?
- What were the factors that led to one team's ten-year dynasty, and how did it all fall apart?
- How could an assassination in 1914 lead almost all of Europe into the massively destructive vortex of a world war?
- How did the messy ending of that war—World War I—lead to the start of World War II?
- What were the factors that led to Donald Trump's surprising election in 2016?
- How did the Middle East become such a violent and conflicted part of the world, and what have been the effects on the rest of the region and the rest of the world?

As you can see, causal arguments are an enormous factor in our daily lives, our politics, our understanding of nature, and our interactions with others.[2]

We also argue about *background causes,* the deeper factors that lead to the phenomena we see today. Scientists study almost nothing but causes; they are interested in how things happen. So they are often interested in these deeper background causes—for instance, of star cluster formation or the runaway cell division that we call cancer. What is leading to a spike in heart disease among middle-aged American men? Do cell phones, cell phone towers, and high-tension lines really cause cancer? Sociologists look at the background causes of inner-city crime, or a jump in white-collar crime; in recent years, many people in psychology, sociology, economics, criminology, and more have been studying the background causes of school shootings, racial tension, and economic hardship.[3]

We also argue about *effects*, about the results of different actions. I just finished reading a book (which I'll discuss later in more detail) that described how the United States' ugly failure in Vietnam led to a complete rethinking of the military... and yet not enough rethinking to prevent us from two more messy conflicts in Iraq and Afghanistan. Many have argued that when the Democrat-controlled Senate rejected Robert Bork's nomination to the Supreme Court in 1987, this led to Republicans' deciding to take the gloves off, and the consequences of this decision are the bitter partisan politics we have today. Life is rarely as simple as one cause leading to one effect and then everything standing still. Quite often we have a chain of causes: A cause leads to a variety of effects, which become causes, which lead to effects, which themselves cause something else...

So as you can see, causal arguments are tricky and complex. I am always telling my son, who completed a difficult electrical engineering major, that electrical circuits are easy; until we get to the quantum level, the electrons do utterly predictable things over and over. I say this whenever he and I are talking about the human body, whose systems, he admits, are much more complex than those of an electrical circuit or even a big computer. Now take many of those individual humans, with their various minds and emotions and desires, and try to figure out how something happened or what might happen next. It can be difficult to separate out all the different factors that led to a given situation.

Consider a causal situation we all think we understand: World War II started when Germany invaded Poland in 1939. But of course many, many factors led Germany to invade Poland that September, just as many, many factors led the Japanese imperial government to mount a surprise attack on Pearl Harbor on December 7, 1941.

So as we begin to work on how to make a sound causal argument, we will have to learn how to tease out these different factors and how to persuade others that *our* understanding of how something came about is the *correct* one.[4]

Talkin' 'bout Causes: The Language and Types of Causes

The first thing we need to do when arguing about causes is to use a particular vocabulary to help us tease out causes and effects—that is, how things happen and why. You may have used some of these terms casually and imprecisely—remember, you already know how to do this—but if you can begin to use them carefully and precisely, you can make crucial distinctions and get at the issues much more effectively.[5]

Proximate versus Remote Causes

Proximate means "nearby" and *remote* means "far away," right? So a proximate cause is one just before the event, the thing that kicked off the final steps leading to the event, while a remote cause is one further back in time. If we think of a "chain of causality," the proximate cause is a link right near the end of the chain, while a remote cause is a link far back in the chain. What was the proximate cause of World War II's outbreak? Hitler's invasion of Poland. What were the remote causes? Most scholars trace those back to the sloppy end of World War I and the failure of the victorious powers to craft a peace agreement that would lead to lasting stability. But of course, you can trace it back to even more remote causes—to the Franco-Prussian War in 1870, or to the need for natural resources, especially coal from the Alsace-Lorraine region, after the Industrial

Revolution. The search for remote causes can be almost endless, but it is also enormously helpful.[6]

Necessary, Sufficient, Precipitating, and Contributing Causes[7]

A *necessary cause* is a factor that must be present for the effect to take place. For instance, any Boy or Girl Scout knows that to have fire, you must have oxygen, fuel, and heat; each of those causes is *necessary* for us to have a fire. Take away any one of those three necessary causes, and the effect—a fire—simply won't happen. Is it necessary to have eleven players on each team to play soccer? No—you can play a fun little soccer game with six, or five, or even three on each team. (The official rules, however, say for a *sanctioned game* to take place, it is *necessary* for each team to have least nine players.)

Sufficient means "enough," so a *sufficient cause* is one that is enough all by itself to make an effect happen. Let's go back to our fire example. It is *necessary* to have oxygen, heat, and fuel to have a fire. But is any *one* of these *sufficient in itself* to make a fire happen? No. So heat, fire, and oxygen are necessary but none of them is a sufficient cause of fire. On the other hand, you have about six liters of blood in your body. If you lose a sufficient amount of blood—around two liters—you will die. Loss of one-third of your blood, then, is a *sufficient* cause of death all by itself.

Fire and loss of blood are pretty simple, however. So let's try a more complex one: Was Adolf Hitler *necessary* for World War II to have happened? That is, without Hitler, would World War II never have happened at all? Now let's ask it a different way: Was Hitler *sufficient* as a cause all by himself to have made World War II happen, or did other factors have to be in place for war to break out?

We can also talk about *precipitating causes*. These are the final steps that, when all the other factors are in place, kick off the actual results. You might think of the precipitating cause as the match that finally gets touched to the powder keg—someone had to buy the gunpowder, store it, bring it together, set up a fuse, buy the match, and bring it to the location, but nothing would have happened until someone struck the match and lit the fuse. The assassination of Archduke Ferdinand in 1914 was one such event. Or let's go back to World War II. It is my understanding—I'm no expert here—that Hitler did not think his invasion of Poland would be the *precipitating cause* of World War II. He thought England and France would acquiesce, appeasing him as they had with Czechoslovakia. Furthermore, he already had a nonaggression pact with the Soviet Union, so he was safe on his eastern flank. But France and England thought he had gone a step too far, and they declared war. (Notice, however, that for the United States, neither the invasion of Poland, nor the blitzkrieg through France, nor the air war over Britain was enough to push the country into war; it took the *precipitating cause* of the attack on Pearl Harbor, more than two years after the attack on Poland, for it to enter the war.) Others have argued that the birth-control pill was the precipitating cause of the sexual revolution in the 1960s; after the pill became widely available, there was no going back.

And this brings us to the fourth kind of cause. *Contributing causes* are those factors that by themselves are neither necessary nor sufficient. They do not have to be there for the event to happen, and they are not enough by themselves to make the event happen. Nor are they the final factors. But they *help* make things happen. While oxygen, heat, and fuel are necessary for fire to start, other contributing factors can help or hinder you from starting a fire. For example, having dry wood contributes to ease in starting a fire, while wet wood might keep you from achieving the heat necessary for fire. A good location, with enough of a breeze (for the oxygen) but not too much wind, might contribute to your success in starting a fire. These are contributing causes.

As I suggested, many factors fed into, or *contributed* to, the outbreak of World War II, even though none was necessary or sufficient in itself to cause the war. There was a whole history of German–French–English–Russian "balance of power" relations going back to the French Revolution and before, and there were wars Germany and France had fought previously. There were the crushing economic sanctions imposed against Germany at the end of World War I, which Hitler blamed for the particularly terrible conditions Germany endured during the worldwide Depression. There was Japan's limited economy and its desire for a larger empire to support itself. And there were of course the larger global movements of national socialism and communism. Japan's sense of its cultural superiority—even its racism—played a role. All of these contributed to the outbreak of World War II, but none was, in and of itself, sufficient, or precipitating, or even necessary, as a cause of the war.

So you can see that distinguishing between what causes are *necessary*, what causes are *sufficient*, what causes are *precipitating*, and what causes are merely *contributing* is extremely important when you are trying to persuade others about the causes and the effects of something.

Hidden Causes

Hidden causes are those that most people either do not know about or don't understand. People may not know about the pollution in a stream or, therefore, the bad effects the pollution has on humans and wildlife. You could bring this cause-and-effect relationship to light. Or you may notice a factor that is leading to a spike in mental illness rates in students that you believe is being overlooked. "Hidden cause" is not really a technical term, because any of the above kinds of causes could be hidden until a good historian, scientist, or investigator brings it to light. But it can help to think about whether you are writing about a cause that is generally known or one that most people do not know about or acknowledge.

Reciprocal Causes

Reciprocal causes are causes that lead back to another cause and then back to themselves again in a loop. For example, most places in the United States fund public schools with property taxes. So more expensive homes generate better property taxes, which lead to better-funded schools, which mean more people want to live in those areas, which drives up house prices, which leads to better funding for schools, which leads to... you get the idea. On the other hand, if an area is even perceived to be sliding—either in quality of schools *or* house prices—people move out, house prices drop, tax revenues go down, the schools lose funding and are perceived to be in difficulty, and demand for housing falls further, leading to poorer funding... again, you can see how quickly this can happen. Reciprocal causes can be fascinating to tease out, as you discover that a cause leads to an effect that itself becomes a cause leading back to the original effect.

Shaping the Argument: How to Create Effective Causal Arguments

As you can see, causal arguments are complex, and teasing out the many factors that led to an effect can be tricky. But ultimately what you are doing is drawing out the *chain of causation*: showing how one event or decision led to another, and then another, tracing this chain of events to show your reader the factors that moved from the cause(s) to the effect(s). So a causal argument rests powerfully on what the classical tradition of rhetoric calls *logos*, or an appeal to logic; you must show with evidence and reasoning how one thing led to another. A second kind of appeal in the classical tradition—*ethos*, or an appeal to the speaker's character—may be important, but only in the sense that you show you are in command of the information. The third kind of appeal—*pathos,* or an appeal to emotion—is much less a factor here, and it may even do you harm. If your audience senses you are too emotional about the subject—or are trying to get them to be emotional about the subject—they might suspect that you will overlook some factors or fudge others to get to the cause or effect in which you seem to be emotionally invested.

So let's think, as Aristotle is always asking us to do, about how ordinarily people argue about causes. What are the tasks you must accomplish to create an effective causal argument?[8]

As I see it, a causal argument must

- Describe fully the phenomenon or event you are concerned with
- Then either
  - Lead us to understand the chain of events that led to this, or
  - Lead us to understand the effects that came out of this
- While also
  - Eliminating false causes, those factors that people may think were part of the chain of causality but in actuality were not

Let's take a look at three patterns or possible organizations for your causal argument:[9]

Pattern 1: Effect Stems from Causes A, B, and C

When you are writing a paper, use this pattern to start with a phenomenon and then work backward into its causes. Often in this kind of argument, the effect is relatively well known and the question is "What is behind this?" For example, what is the cause of cancer of the throat? What is really behind inner-city gun violence? In this case, you start by describing the effect: the sad picture of advanced throat cancer, or statistics (and perhaps a dramatic scene) of inner-city gun violence. Then you work your way backward, tracing out the causes that have produced this situation. (And it just as easily might be a happy effect: why this team was successful, how this beautiful film came to be). Once again you have to follow the chain of causation, either starting with your second paragraph at the fundamental remote moment and then leading back to the effect or tracing a chain of causes backward to the root moment, situation, or cause.

Pattern 2: Cause A Leads to Effect B, Which Causes C, Which Causes D...

This is a good form for when you want to show a series of causes, one leading to the other, which ends up in some more or less final state. For instance, you could argue that a student's excessive partying led to his poor grades. But what were the intermediate steps? Was there a cascade of effects, each becoming a cause of the next step? Did one cause precipitate another and then another? Did contributing causes happen once the student started drinking?

Notice how this same subject matter might work equally well as a Pattern 1 argument: You could start with the student's poor grades and trace it back to his excessive partying...and then maybe beyond that to what caused the excessive partying. But Pattern 2 starts with one step and moves forward into successive effects.

You could also use Pattern 2 to organize an argument I mentioned previously: how the "Borking" of Robert Bork when he was nominated to the U.S. Supreme Court led to Republican anger...which led Republicans to decide not to play nice anymore...which led to a more sharply partisan spirit in Washington, D.C....which got us to our divided national politics today.

To give another example, you might begin with a section describing the messy end of World War I and describe how, step by step, Europe lurched to an even more destructive war in twenty years' time. Did the aftermath of World War I lead to a Germany so wounded and economically devastated that it was open to a figure such as Hitler and all that happened after that? That is one way of explaining this chain of events. But there are other ways. More recently, some historians have argued against the thesis that Allied punishment led Germany back to war; they argue that Germany sought out a war and welcomed acting with greater brutality than ever before.

Pattern 3: Cause A Leads to Effects A, B, and C

Here you have a single cause and try to show the effects (good or bad, or both) that come from it. So, for instance, you could use Pattern 3 to structure the Robert Bork argument. Rather than laying out how one event led to another as in Pattern 2, you argue that one action led to various effects: The "Borking" of his Supreme Court nomination led to Republican anger, to the decision to "take the gloves off," *and* to a more sharply divided partisan politics.

In this template, then, you would start with a paragraph on the initial situation or phenomenon: the Senate hearings on Bork's nomination, what happened there, and how they ended with a vote against his nomination to the Supreme Court. From that you would draw out the way this cause led to the different effects: the anger, bitterness, and change in tactics that both parties adopted. And you must label and explain the different types of causes involved here. How was this cause a necessary or sufficient cause of the effects? Was it a remote or proximate cause? Or did it merely contribute to a situation already in place? Did it precipitate immediate effects? Your paragraphs would tease out how this cause led to these effects and what kind of cause it was.

So as you think about writing your causal argument, you can see three different templates, or standard outlines, for these arguments:

TEMPLATE 2.1
Effect Stems from Causes A, B, C, and D

I. Describe the situation, phenomenon, or event
   a. Again, give a picture. Use statistics (for, e.g., gun violence), descriptive work (putting us on an inner-city street on a Friday night), and/or narrative (an anecdote about math instruction).
   b. Ask: How did we get here? What caused this phenomenon?

II. Explore causes
   a. Depending on the types of causes, you might want to group them:
      i. Which causes were remote and which were proximate?
      ii. Which were the necessary causes?
      iii. Which were sufficient?
      iv. Which were contributing factors?
      v. Was there any precipitating cause?

(Do you need to cover all of these? No. A causal paper might explain that it will explore one particular cause, or type of cause, and leave the rest for some other argument. But the writer might want to know something about all of these causes, even if the argument will focus on just one of them.)

III. Eliminate false causes

TEMPLATE 2.2
Cause A Leads to Effect B, Which Becomes Cause B, Which Leads to Effect C, Which Becomes Cause C, Which Leads to Effect D . . .

I. Describe the phenomenon
   a. You probably want to start at the end of the chain: the ultimate result, e.g., the student's horrible grades leading to his dropping out of college

II. Go back to moment before the most remote cause—before any of the effects had happened
   a. E.g., describe a time when the student was happy and doing well in classes

III. Start with the most remote cause
   a. E.g., the student moved to a new dorm and fell in with a new group of friends who were heavy partiers

IV. Work down the chain of causes and effects, leading back to the phenomenon

TEMPLATE 2.3
Cause Leads to Effects A, B, and C

I. Describe the cause
   a. Give a picture of what happened (or is happening)
   b. Ask: What happened as a result?

II. Describe effect A
   a. Was the cause a contributing, necessary, sufficient, or precipitating cause of this effect?
   b. How can you be sure the cause was a cause of this effect?

III. Describe effect B
   a. Was the cause a contributing, necessary, sufficient, or precipitating cause of this effect?
   b. How can you be sure the cause was a cause of this effect?

IV. Describe effect C
   a. Was the cause a contributing, necessary, sufficient, or precipitating cause of this effect?
   b. How can you be sure the cause was a cause of this effect?

V. And so on, until you have described all the effects you wish to describe (You might want to describe only one effect; that's okay.)

VI. Eliminate false causes/effects, especially if there are popularly held ideas that your research has shown to be wrong

A Quick Note on Research and Its Crucial Place in Causal Arguments

With definitional arguments, you might need to do a little research, to give examples of the subject and predicate, perhaps. But definitional arguments are not usually terribly demanding in terms of research. Causal arguments are different. I know I keep saying this, but causes are complex. It is rare to know a subject or phenomenon so well that you can, just from your own knowledge base, explain all the factors that caused it to come about. (Even if you were there in the dorm and watched the student as he began hanging out at parties and his grades fell, you probably don't know the whole story.) This is where research comes into play: You need more information as you tease out the causes and effects.[10]

But I would encourage you not to confine the term *research* to "reading books in the library" or even "going online and seeing what is there." Those are both good things to do—if the information you gain in books and through Google is relevant and authoritative. But research can and should mean much more. Research might involve interviewing relevant people (those who actually live in the inner city and deal with the situations there), or talking to an expert (universities tend to have these readily available on myriad subjects, so you should not have to look far!), or looking at municipal records and archives. If you are not living close to these things, email and the internet are great helps. Remember, persuasive causal arguments are based largely on logos, and for logos, you need reasons and evidence. I cannot tell you here exactly what kind of evidence you need for whatever your subject is, but I know you will need it, and a lot of it, to make a causal argument stick. And of course the more you show that you are in command of the evidence, the more your ethos comes across as knowledgeable and authoritative on the subject.

A Warning: Causation and Correlation, and Eliminating False Causes

In a causal argument, it is often just as important to eliminate false causes as to argue for what you see as the actual causes. People tend to get all kinds of ideas in their heads about why things happen. Psychologists tell us this is because our brains are wired to seek out causal relationships, probably because this kept us alive when we were running around on the savanna hundreds of thousands of years ago. ("Ah, Gog, I wouldn't eat that kind of berry—the last time I did, I was sick for days.") So part of what you must do in a causal argument is investigate all the causes that people have proposed as behind your phenomenon and ferret out which ones are valid and which are not. We can be fooled by things that look like causes, that feed into our brain's need to seek out causes but are not *actually* causes.

One thing to be particularly careful about is the difference between *causation* and *correlation*; in the latter, things happen together, but one of them does not really cause the other. So, for instance, SAT prep workshops are always claiming that they increase scores by 100, 200, 300, or however many points. Deep dives into the data, however, have failed to prove any direct causal connection. It could be that the students who sign up for such courses are already the type to put in the time and effort and dedication to improve their SAT scores. That is, the clientele for these courses is already self-selected and likely to score better the second time around. The instruction in the classes may not be—seems not to be—the actual *cause* of the improved score at all. The improved score *correlates* with attendance at these workshops but is not *caused by* the workshops. (So are the workshops worth your money? That's your decision.)

Two Ways to "Prove" a Causal Argument

So how can you prove a causal argument to your audience? This can be quite tricky indeed, and it requires a lot of care. But here are two ways[11] that can help seal the deal:

The Single Difference

Let's say there are identical twins raised the same way by the same parents with the same influences and who attend the same schools. They receive the same grades, maybe even go off to the same university, major in the same subjects, and have similar success; sometimes twins even date and fall in love with very similar mates. One ends up an enormously successful millionaire and the other falls into alcohol and drug abuse and destroys his life and ends up in a homeless shelter. What was the *single factor* that distinguished the one from the other? What can we look at to answer this question? Can we find the one influence, the one factor, the one occurrence that happened to the second twin differently from what happened to the first?

So the *single difference* is a powerful way to persuade others about causes. If you can find two or more equivalent situations, or people, or phenomena, and then locate the single difference that accounts for two different results, you can often build a powerful case for your causal argument.[12]

Why are some third-world countries relatively stable and prosperous and others continually in turmoil? Why are some children more successful than others? (One answer suggested in the 1980s was birth order as the single difference; since then this research has been questioned.)

The Common Factor

The *common factor* is the opposite of the single difference. Let's say that scientists find the same phenomenon popping up in seemingly unrelated places among different kinds of people from different walks of life. What is the common factor among all of them? If we can find that common factor, we have probably found the cause of this phenomenon.

This actually happened in 1976, when a new disease, which seemed like pneumonia but was much more dangerous and fast-acting, began popping up all across America. One doctor noticed a pattern, and the Centers for Disease Control and Prevention started investigating almost two hundred cases and twenty-nine deaths. The researchers soon made a connection: All of those infected had attended the same national convention of the American Legion in Philadelphia that July (celebrating the country's bicentennial). Then they narrowed it down further and found a new bacterium (which they later named *Legionella pneumophila*) that had been breeding in the hotel's air conditioning cooling tower and then had blown throughout the hotel. The investigators had found the common factor that had caused the outbreak: a new illness that came to be known as Legionnaires' disease.

A great deal of epidemiological research works through the common factor. When doctors find a cluster of cancer cases—the same kind of cancer in a particular geographical area—they often search for a common factor that could be causing this spike. Perhaps there's a Superfund chemical dump site nearby, or perhaps it is some other factor. In sociology, criminology, and many other fields, the search for the common factor is an important way to understand causes. But it can be tricky to establish the common factor in a complex world where many other factors might be involved as well.[13] (In fact, to take one example, most scientists are not convinced that the evidence shows high-tension wires cause cancer, whereas research has convincingly demonstrated that several Superfund sites caused spikes in cancer nearby.)

So in these two situations, you have two additional templates, each with its own set of tasks to accomplish:

TEMPLATE 2.4
The Single Difference

I. Describe all the commonalities in your two (or three, or however many) subjects
   a. E.g., two brothers: all the things that are alike in them, their upbringing, etc.
II. Describe the different results (or effects)
III. Identify the single difference that led to the different effects, despite all the other commonalities
   a. Show why this single effect caused the difference

TEMPLATE 2.5
The Common Factor

I. Identify the different instances of a single phenomenon
   a. E.g., American Legion members all dying of similar symptoms
   b. Show how different they all seem to be (e.g., geographically) and yet how alike they are in some crucial way
      i. E.g., very different people all with the same disease

II. Identify the common factor that unites all these instances
   a. Argue for this commonality and thus its cause of the phenomenon

Now it's time to try making some of your own causal arguments. But before I do that, let me return to a point from chapter 1...

Is the Old Five-Paragraph Essay Dead Yet? I Hope So

By now you can see that causal arguments work in a completely different way from definitional arguments. They have different parts or, in the language I have been encouraging you to use, different *tasks* to be accomplished. And I hope you see that neither of them fits the model of the old five-paragraph essay. Or to say it a different way: That model doesn't show you how these arguments *really work*, how you need to sequence the subpoints of your argument, or what tasks you need to accomplish in what order. Once you understand that different kinds of arguments need different kinds of organization, you are on your way to making great arguments.

So...can I get the stone carver working on that tombstone? Let me know.

All right. Let's get to work making some of your own causal arguments.

EXERCISES

Exercise 2.1 Working with a partner, brainstorm as many causal arguments as you can. If you get stuck, think about things in your personal life (finances, activities, family history). Consider historical events that fascinate you. If you think you "don't like history," think of the history of an activity you enjoy: baseball, ballet, fashion, woodworking. (Based on my own interest—the sport I have been playing and/or coaching since 1970—I want to write a book someday called *Why Americans Hated Soccer, and How That Changed*.) Think about international events, recent elections, events in your own community, school, or classes. Then ask, "Why did this happen? How did this happen?"[14]

To help you get started, here are some sample causal arguments students have discussed in my classes. (Again, I do not necessarily agree with or endorse these positions.)

- Wearing a helmet may help to prevent Parkinson's disease.
- Marijuana use causes particular harm in adolescents.
- Zombie movies, books, shows, etc., have seen a drastic rise in popularity because of the lack of political education and political community in most modern culture.
- Education in America changed in the 1970s and '80s to reflect a growing concern for technological advancement as a result of the Cold War between the United States and the USSR.
- Mindfulness can effectively break through anxiety's pattern of irrationality.
- Bedtime induces hunger in small children.

- Entitlement creates conflict between teachers and students/parents about grades.
- People do not support the performing arts by purchasing tickets because it is costly to do so.
- Moderating and banning language as a means of preventing offense creates adults unable to cope with the challenges of life.
- Eating candy leads to increased cavities in children.
- Younger drivers lead to higher rates of car accidents.
- Scrolling through Instagram leads to a loss of faith in mankind.
- The arid, intemperate climate has prevented the establishment of a defining culture in Phoenix.
- Increasing the weight that class participation has on a student's grade decreases the quality of discussion.
- Because churches cater to extroverts, introverted members are marginalized.
- Poverty is a contributing and reciprocal cause in addiction and depression.
- Childhood exposure to abuse or household dysfunction can increase a person's risk for several leading causes of death.
- Willpower is the result of the alignment between one's learned and personal values and one's prioritizing right action over pleasure.
- Having Spirit Week and Fall Admissions events in the same week causes undue teacher stress.
- Good leadership can cause positive changes in the atmosphere of an organization.
- Political gridlock in Washington has a number of causes, including increased polarization of the electorate, social media resulting in more extreme views among

commentators, and postmodern culture resulting in a loss of mass culture as a unifying fabric in American life.
- Encouraging everyone to get a college degree diminishes the quality of those degrees.

Exercise 2.2 Using the templates, map out how you would argue one of the causal arguments you just brainstormed. To do this, you will need to think about which of the patterns would fit your argument. Are you starting with a cause and leading to varied effects? Are you starting with the effects and working backward to the cause? Is your argument a good one for looking for the single difference or the common factor?

Also, try to discern which of the kinds of causes you are exploring. Will you say that your cause was a sufficient one? A necessary but not sufficient cause? A precipitating cause? Identifying the kinds of causes you are exploring can give you a structure for your paper.

If you think of all of these as *tasks you need to accomplish* to be persuasive, you will have a good, practical sense of what you must do first, second, third, and fourth.

Work with a partner if it helps. A partner can help you discover causes you might not have considered or alert you to false causes that you will need to set aside.

Exercise 2.3 When you are ready, write up your causal argument. Try your best to describe the phenomenon well and then lead the reader through the causes and/or effects. Eliminate false causes and build to your conclusions about how this phenomenon came to be. Again, focus on how you will need to complete these necessary tasks to persuade your audience, not on "doing what Dr. Roper told me to do."[15]

Humility About Causes and Effects as a Crucial Rhetorical Strategy... and an Acknowledgment of the Truth

It is important, when you're arguing about causes, to acknowledge the complexity that haunts all causal arguments. If you come across as saying that you have all the answers to these complex problems, you risk your readers saying, "Oh yeah? You completely left out these other factors, so I don't find you credible." But if you can suggest that you are aware of the complexity and are giving your best understanding of the situation while acknowledging that other factors might be involved, you often gain by this presentation of your ethos as reasonable, humble, and careful.[16] A good way to do this is to bracket off what you are trying to do: "I'm suggesting that these are contributing causes of *x*, not the only factors," or "I admit that there were many other contributing and even necessary causes of *y*, but this was the precipitating factor that set things in motion," or "I have tried to lay out the main reasons—the necessary and sufficient conditions—for why the Allies were victorious in World War II, but it was a long, complex conflict, and I am fully aware that there were other factors." Or even "I believe I have located the single difference, but it is possible that later evidence will be unearthed that will lead scientists to discover other, crucial causes of this phenomenon."

You might think such humility will undermine your authority, but because causes are so complex, this stance will actually increase your credibility. So these acknowledgments are important to make, probably in your concluding paragraph and perhaps in your introductory one as well, not just because it helps you "win the argument" but also because, well, it's true—and therefore the right thing to do. (If all you want to do is win arguments, I'm not your best guide, nor is Aristotle or anyone coming out of the great classical, medieval, and Renaissance tradition of rhetoric. Those thinkers believed in truth and wisdom, and contrasted themselves with mere sophists, who taught people how to win arguments in order to get ahead in life.)

Further Reflection: Aristotle's Four Causes, the Importance of the Final Cause, and Why a Confused Anthropology Leads to a Confused Education[17]

Aristotle was the first to give us a rational way to think about causes and effects. He talks about four different causes, and these have become fundamental to how we talk about causes and effects. He talks about the *material, formal, efficient,* and *final* causes. As we will see in a moment, most of the time in the modern world we talk about only one of his causes, what he calls the efficient cause. So it is worth our time to explore his more comprehensive sense of causes.

The *material* cause is simply the stuff of which something is made. If you don't have any material, nothing can happen: If you want to carve a piece of wood but have no wood in your workshop, well, you're not making anything that afternoon. So the material *is* a cause—a fundamental one. For a sculpture, the material cause might be the clay or the marble. A computer is made out of wires and transistors and switches. A human is made out of atoms, proteins, cells, all the way up to tissues and organs and organ systems.

The *formal* cause is a little trickier to understand, but it is what forms the raw material into the thing it is. You might say this is the *idea* behind the thing: what idea you have for that piece of wood to turn into before you start carving it, or the concept it took to form that marble into Michelangelo's sculpture of David. Michelangelo had to conceptualize the form to turn the material into that biblical figure. (Michelangelo famously said that he saw the shape inside the block of marble, and that his job was to chip away all the extra material and release the sculpture hiding inside. His unfinished series of *Prigioni* sculptures powerfully evokes his process.) So Michelangelo's form, his idea, is a *cause* of the sculpture—it turns a block of marble into a representation of a person. If the *material* cause of a computer is a set of wires and switches and transistors and such, someone had to have the *idea* of how you put all these things together to form an Apple iPhone—or even the idea that you could put all these things together to create something new called a "smartphone." Steve Jobs had the *idea* that a phone could be more elegant and user-friendly and have far greater capabilities; that idea is what *caused* the iPhone to come into existence. No one else had had that idea before, so Jobs's idea was the formal cause of the iPhone. You could say that DNA contains the code, the idea, for forming a human... but then again, who had the idea to form DNA into that particular code? A theist believes that God had the idea of a human and formed DNA into the code that would physically transmit the idea, just as Steve Jobs had the idea for an iPhone and had engineers and designers produce the technical design.

The *efficient* cause is what we normally think of when we think about causing something: It is the actual movement of the sculptor's hands, the actual making of the computer by assembling the wires and semiconductors and switches into the iPhone or the MacBook. The efficient cause is the action of putting the thing together or making something happen. So I moved my hand and it pushed around a block of spinning clay into the shape of a bowl—that is the efficient cause of molding the material.

Or let's try scoring a goal in soccer. My feet and the leather of the ball are the material cause; the idea of curving the ball around the defender and into the top corner of the net is the formal cause; and the action of my foot contacting the ball at high speed, in just the right spot and just the right way, is the efficient cause. And the final cause is, well, scoring a goal to help my team win the soccer game.

Huh? The final cause? What's that?

The *final cause* is something we do not normally think of as being a cause at all. Aristotle explains that the final clause is the ultimate *purpose* for which the thing is being made, the ultimate reason for which we are acting and causing. Aristotle thinks this cause is enormously important. So if the material cause is a lump of clay, if the formal cause is the idea of the bowl that we want to shape the clay into, and if the efficient cause is moving our hands along with the spinning wheel to shape the lump into that form, then the final cause might be to have a receptacle to hold our food. Note that the final cause is not the bowl itself but the purpose for which the bowl will be used. You don't make a bowl just to make a bowl, right? A bowl has a purpose, a reason for coming into being. This is its final cause.

But we also like it when the bowl has a further final cause—to be a beautiful object in our homes. Any concave object can hold our soup, but we want our bowls to speak to us on the aesthetic level—to be attractive as well as functional.

We can say the same thing about an iPhone or a sculpture. What is the final cause of an iPhone? Well, that's what makes it interesting, right? Steve Jobs saw that a handheld device could have so many more purposes than just voice communication or even text communication; it could be a computer you hold in your hand. It could not serve that final cause, he thought, unless ordinary people, non-techies, could use it easily. But crucially, he also thought it should be attractively designed, elegant, even beautiful. (He learned this from the Italian firm Olivetti, which made portable typewriters and gave them sleek Italian lines, to be beautiful objects in the Italian tradition.) The iPhone didn't *have* to be elegant; other phones before it were more functional and techie in their look, like the Blackberry. But Jobs wanted a phone that would speak to us on the aesthetic level, as his MacBooks and other computers had. Surely this beauty is a large part of the final cause of the iPhone.

This brings us back to our sculpture: What is the final cause of the *David*? Surely Michelangelo was trying to communicate something about Florence as the David against the Goliaths of the rest of Italy. Surely in capturing David in the moment of thought before the battle, he was, the art historians tell us, focusing on the Hero as Renaissance Man in Contemplation. But all of this, I would suggest, is folded into the final, final cause of capturing the beautiful. The beauty of the *David* is the final cause of that sculpture. Isn't it?

If the final cause was so important to Aristotle and to thinkers for centuries to follow, why do we rarely think of it as a cause today? The answer has to do with the explosion of natural science in the seventeenth century. Science is wonderful at explaining material and efficient causes—that is, what something is made of (chemistry) and how it works (physics, biology, etc.). To some extent it also studies formal causes, as when it looks at DNA. So science is great at telling us *how*. But it cannot do much to explain *why*. It cannot really investigate, with its experimental tools, the reason for doing something, so the final cause gradually fell to the side. The rise of science enshrined the idea that explaining material and efficient causes was the only *real* knowledge. When we make causal arguments today, we tend to talk about the hand that moved particular events or the national leaders who caused an event to happen. Or we tend to talk about material causes like aluminum or petroleum as factors in the modern economy. We might talk about the form of a thing, like the beautiful lines of a Ferrari or the design of the new art museum, but we rarely do so in terms of *causes*.

Trained by the new power of science to think about efficient and material causes, and seeing that science couldn't say much about the final cause, we in Western culture began to make what is called the *fact/value distinction*, which says that final causes are a matter of taste. We could talk about supply and demand thoughtfully, but what is a just wage? What is the goal of a human in working in the first place? Science can't tell us anything about that, so, people concluded, those answers must be inaccessible to reason; they must be a matter of opinion. (Strange, though—people had been talking about those things, quite cogently, for millennia.) So we tend to ignore talking about final causes—if they are merely matters of taste, there's no point in discussing them.

But we avoid this crucial Aristotelian concept of the final cause at our peril. John D. Caldwell offers a case study in this danger in his book *Anatomy of Victory: Why the United States Triumphed in World War II, Fought to a Stalemate in Korea, Lost in Vietnam, and Failed in Iraq*. Caldwell's thesis is that in war, generals and political leaders achieve victory when they use "back-to-front thinking": They figure out what the end goal is, then summon all the resources, strategies, and tactics to achieve that goal. That is the approach U.S. leaders followed in World War II, Caldwell says. They had a clear vision—that is, they knew the final cause of all their actions—and worked backward from this end goal. But in every war or conflict since, Caldwell argues, American leaders exhibited "front-to-back thinking": They dealt with the situation in front of them and only later tried to figure out their ultimate goal. In other words, knowing and focusing on the final cause leads to victory; ignoring it, or misunderstanding it, hamstrings one's efforts from the start.

In my own professional world—the university—there is a similar crisis about final causes. With tuition and room and board skyrocketing, people look around at universities, see professors working on their own research but having little contact with actual students, and have begun to ask, "What's the purpose of all this?" And universities struggle to give them an answer, to articulate a final cause for having students pay huge sums for a smorgasbord of classes taught by overworked adjuncts and graduate students. Fortunately, I teach at a university that has a clear sense of our final cause: It is to study truth and justice—*Veritatem, Justitiam, Diligite* is our motto. We at the University of Dallas make clear that truth exists and that the ultimate purpose of an education is to learn the truth and grow in wisdom so we can act justly with our fellow humans. And so we can align our strategies and tactics to this final cause. We have a well-thought-out core curriculum that helps students develop a unified vision of what it means to be educated, to live a full and rich human life, what Aristotle called *eudaimonia*.

But if you don't have an understanding of the final cause of a human being, then you probably cannot organize an education to achieve any final cause. And it is in our schools that I see the worst examples of front-to-back thinking. What is the end goal of a human? Ask a superintendent of a wealthy suburban school district, and I doubt you could get much of an answer. Our culture cannot seem to agree on what humans are for—self-expression? self-actualization? acquiring the most toys and pleasures before death? service to others? What leads to true *eudaimonia*, that "human flourishing" about which the ancient philosophers talked because they saw it as the goal of all human action? Very few people today are willing to entertain this question, to start with it as the "back" from which we then derive the "front" in our educational systems. Why? Because of the fact/value problem, many think that the answers to all those questions are just "opinions."

I'm not criticizing; I feel for educators in school systems that don't start with a clear *anthropology*—that is, a philosophy of the human. If a superintendent went to a modern school board and said, "We're not going to institute any new programs until we have a discussion of a true and full anthropology, and understand what we mean by *eudaimonia*," the board would probably fire the superintendent. So the school leadership is left with limited and confused goals for students—"getting into a college with a great reputation," as if moving on to the next prestige address is what an education is about, or "workforce readiness," as if getting a job is the point of an education.

Both are goals like the "kill count" goals in Vietnam—partial, ill thought out, and achieving no real end. Educational administrators and teachers in such places must feel like army lieutenants in Vietnam, dashing from one firefight to the next, doing a superb job in each exchange but lacking any sense of why they are doing the job or where it is all supposed to lead, and missing any measure of whether they are making real progress.

EXTRA FUN WITH CAUSAL ARGUMENTS

A Classic Causal Argument

Brutus Defending His Decision to Kill Julius Caesar, from Shakespeare's Julius Caesar (3.2.14–36)[18]

Let's have some fun with a classic text again. You may know the story: Cassius has seduced the honorable senator Brutus into participating in the assassination of Julius Caesar, whom the conspirators worried was about to become a tyrant. After the killing, Caesar's body is brought to the Roman Forum. Brutus delivers the following speech to mollify the crowd.

As you read, listen for the causal argument here: What does Brutus say caused him to kill Caesar? What evidence does he give? Does he demonstrate a causal chain of events? What else does he do to justify killing the most prominent (but perhaps most dangerous) leader in Rome on the Ides of March, 44 B.C.?

> Romans, countrymen, and lovers! hear me for my
> cause, and be silent, that you may hear: believe me
> for mine honour, and have respect to mine honour, that
> you may believe: censure me in your wisdom, and
> awake your senses, that you may the better judge.
> If there be any in this assembly, any dear friend of
> Caesar's, to him I say, that Brutus' love to Caesar
> was no less than his. If then that friend demand
> why Brutus rose against Caesar, this is my answer:
> —Not that I loved Caesar less, but that I loved
> Rome more. Had you rather Caesar were living and
> die all slaves, than that Caesar were dead, to live
> all free men? As Caesar loved me, I weep for him;
> as he was fortunate, I rejoice at it; as he was

> valiant, I honour him: but, as he was ambitious, I slew him. There is tears for his love; joy for his fortune; honour for his valour; and death for his ambition. Who is here so base that would be a bondman? If any, speak; for him have I offended. Who is here so rude that would not be a Roman? If any, speak; for him have I offended. Who is here so vile that will not love his country? If any, speak; for him have I offended. I pause for a reply.

As you discuss this argument with your classmates, think about the various kinds of causes: which ones does Brutus use in explaining the steps that led him to kill Caesar? Should we be persuaded by this argument, as the crowd apparently is? (One even suggests that they make Brutus into a Caesar.) If so, why? If not, what would it take to persuade you?

You might then turn to Marc Antony's speech, which follows Brutus's. Does Antony offer a causal argument, and if so, how? What about his argument turns the crowd against the conspirators, and can you understand that success in definitional or causal terms?

CHAPTER THREE

EVALUATIVE ARGUMENTS

Is it good or bad?

If we reach agreement about definition—about what something is—and then reach agreement about causes—what caused it or what effects it had—we might need to stop and discuss and argue (that is, reach stasis) at the level of evaluation. Here we are asking the question "Is it good or bad?" You might expand that language to ask, "Is it worthwhile or not worth our time?" "Is it superb or just pretty good?" These are the questions of *evaluation.*

So let's go back to our fight outside the bar.[1] We established that this was assault, and we figured out what caused it (an argument over one man talking with another man's wife) and what effects it had (a broken nose, a mild concussion, hospital expenses and time away from work, etc.). You would think that the next step in our stasis theory journey would be easy: Obviously, it's a bad thing to break another person's nose, right? But maybe not. Maybe there were witnesses who thought the guy with the broken nose "had it coming to him," because of his drunken obnoxiousness that night, or perhaps from seeing a pattern of his behavior over many nights at this particular bar. It could be that he was threatening others, or had actually assaulted someone, and needed to be stopped, perhaps violently, if he could not be stopped any other way. The witnesses might even look up to the puncher as a kind of defender of virtue for putting this Obnoxious-Flirter-with-Other-Men's-Wives, or even Aggressive-Sexual-Harasser-or-Assaulter, in his place. So *even if they conceded the definitional and causal arguments*, they might, by evaluating the punchee as a jerk, evaluate the punch as a good action—in which case, the two sides would again reach stasis and have to argue, to work out their differences.[2]

And of course—you knew I was going to say this, right?—we argue about evaluations all the time. We are constantly making judgments about the quality of the things, people, and events around us. Evaluations are the core of nearly every argument in every sports bar in America:

- Is this quarterback doing a good job or not?
- Is that pitcher worth his enormous salary?
- Is this coach a good coach, or just one who got lucky by having superb players on his team?
- Was that a good play to call in that situation?

Evaluations move well beyond sports. We evaluate—and read reviews (others' evaluations) of—restaurants and films:

- Is that new French bistro any good, or is it just a pretentious, overpriced trap with average food?
- Where can I get a good fish taco in this town?
- Is Martin Scorsese's new movie worth twelve bucks to see it in the theater, or should I wait for it to come out on Netflix?
- Are the dogfights in the original *Top Gun* worth the wooden dialogue and dumb love story?
- In what order do you rank the *Star Wars* movies?

We evaluate music:

- Where does Stevie Ray Vaughan rank on the list of top guitarists of all time?[i]
- Is the new album by the Flaming Lips any good, or are they still in a slump?
- Which is better: this conductor's version of Mahler's Fifth Symphony or the other one's?

Grades are nothing more or less than a teacher's evaluation of his or her students' work during the term. But often students evaluate their teachers at the end of a term as well. Supervisors evaluate their employees for promotion; investors evaluate the worth and future potential of a company whose stock they are considering buying. We are constantly asking the question, "Is this a good thing or a bad thing?" It is important in our daily lives to know whether something is worth our time, our money, or our emotional investment. What do we do when we look online for a product or service? We read the reviews at sites like Yelp and check how many gave this cell phone service, this auto repair shop, this electronic thingamajig five stars or one, whether people had a good experience with this business or a terrible ordeal. We are constantly engaged in the process of evaluation.

But spend five minutes on Yelp, or any other site with product reviews, and you tire of the imprecise, unfocused, emotional, or biased evaluations you find there. Reviewers judge products and services for failing to be something they never pretended to be in the first place (well, no, that's an airplane, sir, not a flying luxury hotel),

---

i If you're interested, a *Rolling Stone* panel of guitar experts in 2015 ranked SRV twelfth, and another poll I saw ranked him seventh. But that gets us into the whole question of expert opinion, which we will discuss in a moment.

for tiny failings that are immaterial to the main qualities (yes, there's a tiny scratch in the back, but it washes your clothes really well and the price is incredible), and for personal slights they imagined ("the waiter strongly recommended the flour tortillas, but I'm celiac—I was so offended!"). And frankly, many of the reviews are not terribly helpful: "This product stinks" is not much of an evaluation.

So since we do this all the time, how can we do it better? How can we think through our evaluations so that they are accurate representations of reality (that is, that they convey the truth)? How can we effectively convey these evaluations to others (that is, persuade them of the truth that we see)? How can we lead others to see the good or the bad in the things we are exploring?[3]

How to Create Effective Evaluative Arguments

If you think about it, the structure or *dispositio* of an evaluative argument is quite simple. The thesis statement looks something like this:

> Yo-Yo Ma is the greatest cellist of all time.[ii]

Notice immediately how easy it is to confuse a definitional thesis with an evaluative one—both have a subject and a predicate linked by a state of being verb: "*x* is *y*." But the evaluative argument has that qualitative adjective ("the greatest") that makes all the difference. You are not answering the question "What is this?"—to which your answer would be "Yo-Yo Ma is a cellist." You are answering a different question: "Is he a good cellist or a bad one?"

And it's not too difficult to figure out what you need to do to persuade someone of this statement, right?

---

ii "Oh, boy," I hear you say. "Better than Pablo Casals? Are you crazy?" But now the fun begins, as we sit around and argue about which one of these utterly transcendent artists is the best ever.

- You must describe the subject well enough that your audience will know what you are evaluating;
- You must lay out clear criteria for judging this thing, person, experience, or concern;

And then

- You must show whether or not the subject measures up to the criteria.

So you need to describe Yo-Yo Ma's cello playing to your readers; you have to set up your judgment (that he is the best); you must set out the standards by which you judge him the best; and you must show that he fits those standards better than anyone else (even better—whew!—than Pablo Casals, which in my book is going to be difficult but maybe not impossible).

But before you explore how to do these things, you have a big set of questions to take on.

Do You Have the Authority to Make Evaluative Arguments?

In the realm of evaluations, we do not live in a radical democracy where everything and everyone is equal. I am sorry if this offends you, but some people's evaluations are worth more than others'. You act on this truth every day of your life. In evaluations, we do, and should, give much more credence to those with authority in the area we are considering, and much less credence to those with little or no authority on the subject. So in classical rhetorical terms, if causal arguments lean heavily on logos, evaluative arguments combine their need for logos with a healthy attention to ethos.

For instance, if we were evaluating the great classical pianists of the twentieth century and I said to you, "Vladimir Ashkenazy was the twentieth century's greatest pianist," would you accept my evaluation? I hope not, because I don't know much about playing the piano or about the classical piano repertoire; I honestly can't name more than a few twentieth-century classical pianists ("um... there's Arthur Rubinstein and... oh yeah, Glenn Gould, who did all the Bach stuff—I've heard of him. After that...?")

If we were evaluating the best and worst NFL quarterbacks, would you listen to me, an English professor who has never played football competitively, or would you listen to a coach with twenty-five years of NFL experience? Let's push this even further: Would you listen to a coach who spent all his time coaching the defensive line or someone whose known specialty was quarterbacks? I hope the answers are obvious here.

Now when it came to evaluating Middle English literature, especially the works of Chaucer and the *Gawain*-Poet, would you listen to the NFL coach or me, who has thirty years of experience reading, writing about, and teaching the English literature of the fourteenth century? But let's go a step further. About that same subject, should you listen to me, who has published a few articles about these authors, or an Oxford University professor who has published six books about Chaucer and his works? Again, I hope the answer is obvious.

The point here is that *those with deeper knowledge of and longer experience in a subject are more worthy of our respect and attention when it comes to evaluating that subject.* They have much greater *authority*, born of this knowledge and experience, to make sound judgments about whether something in their subject area is good or bad. Again, we all know this. Authority has been deeply questioned, even rejected, throughout modernity, but in wider culture this rejection ramped up in the 1960s. *Authority* became almost a curse word in our culture, probably because it gets mistaken for and blended together with *authoritarianism*, which means the abuse of authority, or the assumption of authority by someone who does not possess true authority. But true authority is a wonder to behold: It is the possession of the knowledge, skill, ability, and wisdom to see accurately and judge prudently about a subject.[4] We see it in the simple farmer who knows more about the ways of nature, his livestock, and his crops than any smarty-pants PhD; we see it in the grandfather who commands the respect even of the rebellious teen because of his kind, patient, but deeply virtuous understanding of human nature and thus his treatment of others.

It is not only the old who have the authority to offer persuasive evaluations. Even if you are a relatively young student, I guarantee that in some areas you have much more knowledge, experience, and authority than I do. If you have been practicing a martial art since you were eight; if you have taken lessons in classical piano since you were seven; if you've been a dancer, on a lacrosse team, or in a klezmer band; if you knit; if you grew up on a farm and worked with your parents raising pigs or cattle or soybeans, I can tell you right now you are much more of an expert and can make much better judgments about those subjects than I, who know almost nothing about any of them. So let's set aside the notion that everyone's evaluations, everyone's judgments of the worth or quality of something, are equal. Some people's evaluations are simply more authoritative, and properly carry more weight, than others' do.

This truth sometimes upsets people who have absorbed an ethos of "everyone's entitled to his opinion." If you see a film and like it, you can get upset at the reviewer who said it was not an accomplished piece of film art, and the tendency is to knock the reviewer rather than reconsider your opinion of the film. "Artsy-fartsy idiot," you might say to yourself; "I thought it was great." Or say you have a nice meal at a restaurant and then read a review that trashes the place. "Foodie snob," you might think. Or you pay a ridiculous amount of money to see a concert, have a great time, and the next day read the reviewer's opinion that it was a flat, uninspiring performance whose spectacle drew people's attention away from the mediocre musicianship. "Those guys rocked," you might think, and here's this superior writer-critic-type spoiling your fun. But every year that reviewer goes to many more restaurants, or sees hundreds more films, or attends dozens more concerts, than you do. That critic has studied film technique and structure and knows a great deal about acting and so has vastly more knowledge on which to base his judgments. It's not his one big concert of the year, so he has more data points for comparison. He can therefore be more objective, more sensible, more prudent in his judgments. *His opinion counts more than yours does.*

Does that mean you have to agree with him every time? Of course not. The nice thing about living in a country where the First Amendment enshrines the right to free speech is that you have a right to your own judgment about the film or the concert. This is 'Merica, after all, and I am so, so happy that it is.

And can even an experienced, knowledgeable person get it wrong? You betcha. No one at first thought much of Vincent van Gogh's paintings—he sold only a couple in his lifetime, right? Now every time a van Gogh goes on the market, it seems that it breaks records for the most paid for a painting. No NFL scout thought Tom Brady was worth the NFL's time when he was leaving college, so the New England Patriots drafted him in the sixth round, after 198 other players. Seven Super Bowl rings later, almost everyone in the country considers Brady the greatest quarterback ever to play the game, and he was still playing at an incredibly high level in his forties.

We might have a particular crisis of "expertise" today when political conformism and ideology shape so many supposed experts' judgments, and when our experts have had such an inferior education themselves. And an expert's own worldview can blind him from seeing the genius of those outside of his world. (Expertise comes from technical knowledge but also from a broad-based understanding of human nature and culture.) But the fact that "the experts" sometimes get things wrong does not change the reality that, more often than not, those with knowledge, skill, and experience in a subject get it right, and we do listen to and respect their judgments. (And the van Goghs and the Tom Bradys are by far the exceptions, which is why we notice them; most "great ones" are actually acclaimed fairly quickly. People recognized right away that Bach, Beethoven, Mozart, Milton, Shakespeare, Dante, Johnny Unitas, Hank Aaron, Pelé, and Roberto Clemente were great.)

So maybe the correct question is, how can you effectively enter into the arena of making evaluations? That is, how can you create your own evaluations that will be persuasive? How can you get better at articulating, setting up, and exploring your evaluations?

Let's get to work on creating persuasive evaluations.

Shaping the Argument: How to Create Effective Evaluations

So you want to convey to someone your judgment about a film, a restaurant, a concert, a program, or anything else. What is the first step? *You have to describe the phenomenon.* You will need to introduce the reader to the restaurant, the film, the performance, the situation. Here you will need to bring out all of your descriptive skills, setting the thing before your reader. You need to tell us a bit about the restaurant—what it is, its name, the type of food, the feel and ambience of the place. You might talk about the decor of the restaurant, the way the rooms and tables are prepared, the music playing quietly over the speakers, and of course convey something of the menu. Or in a film review, you might begin by giving your readers enough of the plot and direction of the film (without giving away any spoilers) to entice them to be interested in this particular film.

Other important things are going on in this opening section as well:

- As you describe, you must show that you *know the subject intimately*. Readers do not trust an evaluator who has only cursory knowledge of the subject. A restaurant reviewer makes multiple visits to a particular locale before writing a review. You might need to research the history of a place. You will need to know something about the actors or director or making of a film, and see it more than once, taking notes as you go. Once again, research—in the broadest sense of the term—is a powerful tool in your kit; use it thoughtfully.
- And therefore, you must *establish your authority to speak about this subject*, or readers will question your judgment and possibly stop reading altogether. Establishing your authority is a delicate process, but mostly it depends on demonstrating your knowledge and experience with the subject. It is not a matter of saying explicitly, "I studied classical dance in Paris for twenty-six years under the great…"; it is more a matter of weaving in your knowledge of the terms and concepts of your subject. If you are reviewing the latest Scorsese film and it becomes clear that you have never seen any of this well-known director's other films, or know little about his way of making films, your review is simply not going to be credible. You cannot offer an evaluation of a recent classical music concert and betray in the first paragraph a confusion between Bach and Beethoven, or say that Schubert wrote Mozart's *Don Giovanni*. But if you show that you know the lingo of your subject, that you have command of the language and concepts of cooking or martial arts or offensive line play,

then you instantly become credible; you gain authority in your readers' eyes. During this opening section or paragraph, however long it takes, incredibly important things are happening and you must do them successfully, describing your subject, adding in your knowledge of the subject and its background, and using intelligently the terms and important issues in the subject.

- Third, you must be showing that you are, as much as possible, *a fair and objective judge*. The point is not scientific neutrality—we want an evaluator to have opinions—but if it is clear that you are significantly biased, either for or against your subject, you will not be credible. If it is clear that you hate the New England Patriots and always have, or that you have been a lifelong fan who simply adores everything about them, then your evaluation of their quarterback or coach will suffer in readers' eyes. If you make it clear you think that heavy metal is just loud noise, or that country music is just stupid stuff for hicks, or you won't hear of anyone saying anything against Italian food, then you lose your authority in talking about those subjects.[iii] [5]

Next, you must *offer a judgment*; in other words, you must state your evaluative thesis: Is this thing good or bad? Of course, the answer does not have to be as stark as that, and rarely is. No restaurant is perfect; no film is perfect; no performance of a Rachmaninoff piano concerto is perfect. So a good, thoughtful, authoritatively anchored judgment is often going to be qualified:

---

iii On the other hand, announcing a bias and then showing that you are reversing it in this case is a great way to earn points for objectivity: "I have never really liked Thai food all that much, but this was the best meal I've had in months" or "I scarf any Italian food on any plate at any time, but the meal I just had at Trattoria Luigi was simply horrible."

- Mr. Tanner's presentation of the Schubert *Lieder* Saturday night was a fine evocation of German lyric mastery, but his voice lacked something of the full color necessary to convey the composer's intentions for this cycle.[6]
- Scorsese's film *Raging Bull* demonstrates clearly the director's absolute technical mastery and his usual emotional power, but for all that, I still find his view of the American man limited and stifling.

Now, how do you convince others of your judgment? *You must lay out the criteria for your judgment and show that the subject fits (or doesn't fit, in a negative evaluation) these criteria.*

Actually, if you have gotten to this stage in your evaluation, you surely already have been thinking in terms of your criteria, even if implicitly. (Notice how in the thesis statements above, the writer implies the criteria used in judging the subject.)[7] You already have in your mind criteria for restaurants, and you couldn't have come up with a judgment without having them. You know—even if in an unfocused way—what you like and dislike in films, or you could not have had an opinion about which *Star Wars* film, or which version of *Little Women*, is the best. Of course, you do this all the time. But you are trying to engage in thoughtful, well-considered, articulate, persuasive rhetoric, so you will need to be more precise about your criteria.

What are criteria? How do you find them and establish them?[8] If you are reviewing a seafood restaurant, you do not only talk about this one restaurant. You want to compare this restaurant against the standards you have for all other seafood restaurants, right? And then you might want to compare this restaurant not only to other seafood restaurants but to all restaurants in general. So to find criteria, you step up to a more general category to which your subject belongs.

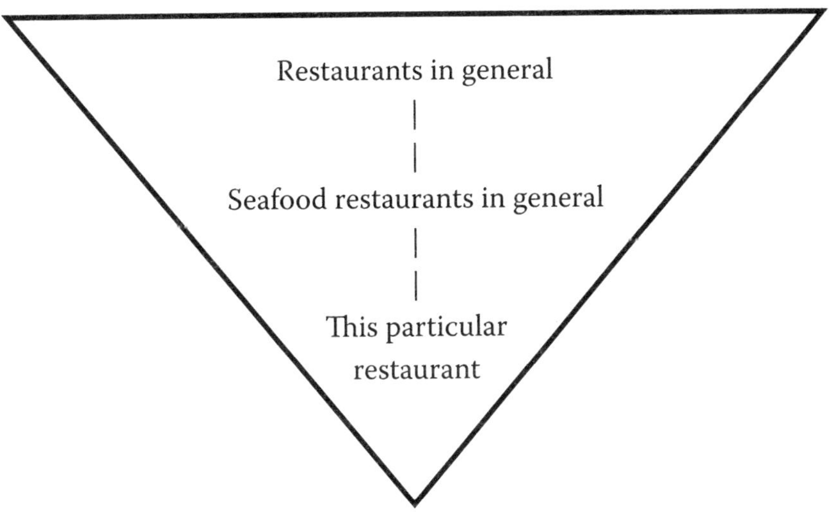

So what makes for a good seafood restaurant in general? Well, the fish should be fresh. And it should be prepared in an interesting way that brings out the flavors natural to the fish. But the restaurant should serve more than fish, right? Shouldn't it have clams, oysters, and crabs as well? Or is that important? *These standards for the general product, place, or phenomenon then become your criteria.* Next you might move to a more general set of criteria: What makes for a good restaurant, period? Here you might talk about not just the menu but also the decor, the service, the ambience, and so on.

The same might go for films. You want to talk about a particular horror film, so you need to go up one level and think about what are your standards for a good horror film. And then you might want to think about what makes a good film in general. Can this film stack up against the best horror films—that is, against the best in its genre? And can it stack up against the great films in other genres?[iv]

iv Notice that my categories might still be too broad here. There are plenty of categories of seafood restaurant between this particular restaurant and "seafood restaurants in general": the Cajun po' boy/shrimp/down-home place, the upscale seafood fancy-fine-dining place with fresh oyster bar, the side-of-the-road fried catfish joint. It's up to you at which level you would like to make the comparison. (For the record, I like each of these immensely if they are done right.)

Again, notice that you're judging a particular thing—this restaurant, this film—by criteria a step up in generality.

But it could be that you do not want to move to the ultimate level of generality in your subject. You might not want to compare a burrito spot with the haute-cuisine French restaurant downtown; that might not be your point. It might even be silly to expand to the general level—the best restaurants in your city—in a review of a burrito joint. Similarly, you might not want to compare the slasher horror film to an art-house film that is trying to do very different things artistically. You might just want to talk about horror films and how this one provides the thrills and chills you seek in this type of movie. A burrito restaurant isn't trying to do the same things that the French restaurant is; surely these restaurants should be judged in different ways and by different criteria. And of course the criteria you use depend on your intentions and your readership. If all you are trying to do is establish that this burrito fast-food chain is better than the other one, and encourage people who want a good, quick burrito to choose the right one, there is no point in comparing it to Chez Gregoire downtown.[9] In none of the other three kinds of arguments is your particular rhetorical intention and judgment so important as in evaluations—and here is where your knowledge, experience, and authority come into play.

From here, it should be obvious what you must do: *Lay out the criteria one by one, and show that the subject fits (or doesn't fit) those criteria.* The criteria will dictate what evidence you use: the technique, and then the expression, of the classical pianist; the food and service and ambience at the restaurant; the skill and power and tactical moxie of the quarterback.

The Evaluative Argument Template

So now you should be able to see the fundamental template for an evaluative argument:

I. Describe the subject
    a. Give a sense of the subject (without giving everything away)
    b. Establish your authority by using the terms and concepts of this field
    c. Establish yourself as a fair and objective judge
II. Offer a judgment (that is, your thesis)
    a. Answer the question, is it good or bad?
    b. Qualify your judgment as necessary
III. Show that the subject fits the criteria
    a. Criterion 1
        i. How it fits this criterion
    b. Criterion 2
        i. How it fits this criterion
    c. Criterion 3
        i. How it fits this criterion
    d. Criterion 4[v]
        i. How it fits this criterion

And so forth, until you have used all of your criteria.[vi]

IV. Answer any remaining counterarguments against your judgment

How Explicit Must the Criteria Be? Do You Need to Establish Them?

Do you need to state the criteria explicitly? Must you make a point of saying what makes for a good restaurant or a good film? It depends—on your readers and on your relationship with them.

---

v I cannot resist saying this again: Do you notice that there are not necessarily three body paragraphs here? There is no magical number; you might have four criteria, or three, or six, for a good table saw, or a good opera singer, or a good elementary school science curriculum.
vi Quick note in case you found these terms confusing: *Criterion* is singular; *criteria* is plural.

Often you can assume that your readers share many, if not all, of your standards. Few people would challenge the idea that a good film should have good acting, well-written dialogue, a coherent plot, and good visuals, sound, and music. So there's no point spelling out these criteria in a movie review; reviewers assume these things and implicitly build the sections of their reviews around them. And when you are writing to experts, or at least knowledgeable people, in a particular field, you probably don't need to spend time going over the criteria. Knowledgeable wine people know what makes for a good wine; you wouldn't spend time writing in *Wine Spectator* setting out the criteria that readers of that magazine have had in their heads for years. On the other hand, when you are an expert explaining things to the general public, you must help educate your readers about how to judge the good from the bad.

Other times, the criteria might not be clear, or widely accepted, and you will need to establish them. My son watches a YouTube channel where three special effects experts play film clips and evaluate whether the effects are good or bad, artful or artless, hilariously weak or exciting and thrilling. But since they know that most of their viewers are not professional effects artists, they explain how these effects work to help us understand good work from poor. And that's fascinating; it helps you know more about what is going on to create the magic that is a great film, and it helps you judge the good from the bad when you watch special effects in other films.

When you are taking a contrarian viewpoint, you will need to establish, and even argue for, your criteria: "This quarterback may not be the most accurate passer, but that is not what is most important here; we should consider *x*, *y*, and *z* as well as, or even instead of, his accuracy." In that case, it is important for the writer to establish *x*, *y*, and *z* as more important criteria for an NFL quarterback than accuracy, which is usually a baseline standard for making it as a starting quarterback. If you are going to say a wine is not complex and rich in its taste, you surely will need to establish what other criteria you are using to rate the wine highly and why those criteria are valid. I will never forget sitting at the Center House, a grungy, wonderful old fried fish shack outside of Green Lake, Wisconsin, listening to five octogenarians play polka music, and a friend saying, "This place is so great that I'd been coming here for five years before I realized I didn't like the food." There's a man who had realized that his usual baseline criterion for a good restaurant—excellent food—simply did not apply in this case. (And I agreed.)[vii]

Evidence for Evaluative Arguments

What sort of evidence works for evaluative arguments? Since you do this all the time, my guess is that you already know that the evidence for evaluative arguments is varied but not mysterious. *First, you need good examples*, and you need to *describe those examples well*: the dishes at the restaurant, the timbre and range of the soprano's voice, the beautifully directed and acted scene that brought the entire film together. Some of this might get technical, as you describe what makes Glenn Gould's playing of Bach better than anyone else's, and so again you will have to judge your readers' ability to understand and engage with such technical details. *You may need factual evidence and statistics*: the passing yards and completion percentages for a quarterback, the album sales for a pop singer. But be careful: Quantitative evidence is rarely fully persuasive when making a qualitative argument, or else we would all think that Michael Jackson's *Thriller* is the greatest album of all time.

vii I still lament the demise of Club Schmitz, a Texas roadhouse with all the grungy charm of the Center House, plus a great shuffleboard table, waitresses who called you "hon," a wonderful jukebox featuring the likes of Ray Charles, *and* great burgers, onion rings, and chili. You were as likely to find a beaten-down pickup truck full of construction workers as a BMW in the parking lot, and these types mixed easily inside. It was a University of Dallas hangout for more than four decades, and I have added this footnote here only so I could offer my evaluation of it as one of the coolest places ever in Dallas and thereby in some small way preserve its memory. *Sic transit gloria.*

Combining the First Three Kinds of Arguments

One of the fascinating things about stasis theory is that you begin to see how learning well the first two types of arguments pays enormous dividends in mastering the latter two types. For instance, you may need to make a definitional argument to make terms clear in an evaluative argument. What actually is a slasher film? How would you define hip-hop as opposed to rap so as to set it apart from other kinds of music and judge it on its own terms? And often a causal argument leads into an evaluative judgment: This activity or situation led to results that were good, or another set of actions led to results that were not good at all. A change in curriculum might have led to higher grades, achievement, and student happiness, and therefore you might judge it to be a good move by the administration.

You might want to argue that Jane Austen was the greatest early nineteenth-century novelist and show that she became so because of the way she absorbed the lessons of medieval romance,[viii] the sentimental novels of the late eighteenth century, and an Aristotelian ethics of virtue.[ix] So you could first make a causal argument to show how these other texts influenced her, and then an evaluative argument showing how this is the basis for her greatness: not so much technical innovation as thematic depth and range of issues. Or if you wanted to turn to popular music, you could offer a causal argument about how Elvis Presley became the King of Rock and Roll by bringing African American music to mainstream white audiences, and then build into an evaluation of his greatness—not just that he created these effects but also that he did them better than anyone else had. Or you could start with a causal argument and then turn to a negative evaluation: You might admit that building a six-story

viii This is the subject of a marvelous doctoral dissertation by Tiffany Schubert, "A History of Happy Love: Happy Endings in Medieval Romance and the Novel," University of Dallas, 2016.
ix See Kathryn E. Davis's wonderful *Liberty in Jane Austen's "Persuasion"* (Lehigh University Press, 2016).

parking garage on campus would add hundreds of parking spaces for students (causal argument) but then pivot to arguing that these beneficial causes do not outweigh the aesthetic catastrophe of erecting such an ugly edifice on a bucolic campus (evaluative argument).

By seeing how you can stack these arguments one upon another, you begin to see how to make sophisticated, compound arguments that do justice to our complex world. In other words, you can get at the truth of things in more refined ways. But it is best to master each of the Four Arguments in isolation first, so you know how each one works. (We will work on combining them in chapter 5.)

EXERCISES

Exercise 3.1 Brainstorm subjects for an evaluative argument. My guess is that this time subjects will come to you rather easily: films, restaurants, products, podcasts, businesses—all those things that get reviewed on the internet. Then turn to things in your local community: the library, a community center, an annual festival or event. Again, you can always think of hobbies and activities (kayaking, quilting, cooking, Irish tin whistle playing) that you know well, for your knowledge, skill, and experience in these areas provide you with authority to offer your judgment. (If you have engaged in an activity like this for a few years, you already have opinions about what is good and bad in that area and probably don't mind sharing those opinions with people who share your passion for it.)[10] Go ahead and offer a preliminary judgment about the subject.

I doubt you will need the help this time, but here are some evaluative arguments my students have made in the past:

- Misty May-Treanor is the best women's volleyball player of all time.[11]
- A two-party political system is worse than a multiparty system.[12]
- Disney movies are among the most psychologically and emotionally damaging children's movies.[13]
- Disneyland really isn't "the happiest place on earth."[14]
- An education based in the liberal arts is better for the soul than a practically based education.[15]
- In most cases, brain surgery that is minimally invasive is the best option.[16]
- Churches that find ways to cater to both extroverts and introverts are better stewards of the Christian message.[17]

Exercise 3.2 Using the evaluative argument template (see pages 88–89), map out how you would argue for your evaluative judgment.[18]

- Consider how to describe your subject: How will you give enough of an introduction so that your readers will understand this topic and be ready to hear your judgment?
  - In that regard, you already need to be thinking about who your readers will be. Are you talking to other experts, or are you presenting this subject to neophytes who will need much more introductory material?
- How will you establish your authority to speak on this subject (without merely listing your credentials), and how will you signal that you are a fair and objective judge?
- How will you offer your judgment? Will it be a bold statement, or will you carefully qualify your judgment?
- What criteria will you use? What standards are usually used for this subject? Do you want to use them, modify them, or include some unusual criteria? Will you need to establish and argue for these, or can you expect your readers to share your criteria?
- What evidence will you produce to show that the subject fits (or does not fit) the criteria? Will you use examples, comparisons, definitions, causes and effects, statistics, the views of experts?

Work through these questions and begin to organize your argument according to the template.

Exercise 3.3 When you are ready, write up your argument, focusing on accomplishing the tasks step by step. Work on offering your readers a good introductory description of the subject. Then make a judgment (that is, your thesis), and take on the criteria one by one, persuading your readers that these are good criteria and that your subject measures up (or does not measure up) to these criteria. Handle counterarguments either as they come up for each criterion or at the end of the argument in one block.

Critical Reading Skills and the Four Arguments

Educators talk constantly about "critical thinking skills" these days; some seem to have no other goals for an education than having students master these mysterious "skills," though most of the time they cannot really explain what they mean by them.[x] But the Four Arguments will help your critical thinking in practical ways.

One of the great things about learning the Four Arguments and their templates is that they give you a standard against which to measure other people's essays, theses, and even oral arguments. Since you now know *what tasks each kind of argument must accomplish*, you can critically evaluate whether the writer has accomplished those tasks. Here, in evaluative arguments, you have important measures for evaluating whether the writer has been effective, persuasive... truthful. Did he use intelligent criteria, the right ones for this subject? Did he establish those criteria, or are they widely enough accepted that you give him a pass on establishing them? How well did he show that the subject measures up to those criteria? Did he entertain and answer any counterarguments against his case? You see, the template takes the guesswork out of critically evaluating an argument. You simply measure whether the writer accomplished the tasks that anyone engaged in this kind of argument must complete to be successful.[19]

---

x Don't believe me? Try it. Ask a school superintendent to explain what he or she means by "critical thinking skills." You will watch the superintendent stumble, or you will hear such ambiguous terms that none of his or her claims could help an actual student do better thinking. The problem is that you can't think in the abstract; you have to think *about something*. So teaching "thinking skills," critical or not, without anything to think *about*, is hopeless. But that's an argument for another book.

EXTRA FUN WITH EVALUATIVE ARGUMENTS

A Classic Evaluative Argument

Hamlet's "To be or not to be" (3.1.64–96)[20]

You have heard at least the first line of this speech before, and many think of it as a speech contemplating suicide. But let's look at it in a different way, as an evaluative argument. Hamlet is asking, "Which is nobler?" That is an evaluative question. Is it good or bad, better or worse, compared to . . . what?

Analyze Hamlet's speech as an evaluative argument. What are his criteria? What evidence does he produce to show his subject fitting those criteria or falling short of them? What, eventually, is his thesis—which is nobler? Or does he end with a different thesis entirely?

To be, or not to be—that is the question:
Whether 'tis nobler in the mind to suffer
The slings and arrows of outrageous fortune,
Or to take arms against a sea of troubles,
And by opposing end them. To die, to sleep—
No more—and by a sleep to say we end
The heartache and the thousand natural shocks
That flesh is heir to—'tis a consummation
Devoutly to be wished. To die, to sleep—
To sleep, perchance to dream. Ay, there's the rub,
For in that sleep of death what dreams may come,
When we have shuffled off this mortal coil,
Must give us pause. There's the respect
That makes calamity of so long life.
For who would bear the whips and scorns of time,
Th' oppressor's wrong, the proud man's contumely,

The pangs of despised love, the law's delay,
The insolence of office, and the spurns
That patient merit of th' unworthy takes,
When he himself might his quietus make
With a bare bodkin? Who would fardels bear,
To grunt and sweat under a weary life,
But that the dread of something after death,
The undiscovered country from whose bourn
No traveler returns, puzzles the will
And makes us rather bear those ills we have
Than fly to others that we know not of?
Thus conscience does make cowards of us all,
And thus the native hue of resolution
Is sicklied o'er with the pale cast of thought,
And enterprises of great pith and moment
With this regard their currents turn awry
And lose the name of action.

Have some fun discussing this text. You might ask, "What is Hamlet actually evaluating?" What is his view of life that he evaluates things in this way? Perhaps reading the speech in this way will reveal things that you have not considered before.

CHAPTER FOUR

PROBLEM/SOLUTION ARGUMENTS

What should be done about this?

We have come to the last of the Four Arguments. With our bar fight, or more accurately, our arguments about it, we have gone through defining what actually happened, seeking the causes that brought about the broken nose, and then judging whether the punch was a good thing or a bad thing. We can imagine a situation where there is little disagreement about any of these things, and where the case moves quickly through the arrest, investigation, indictment, and trial. But we can also imagine, and as we have worked through these chapters, have imagined, a situation where each of these stages produced stasis—a moment where the two sides disagreed, so we had to stop, consider, and debate a particular question: What actually was that? What caused it and what were its effects? Was that punch a good thing or a bad thing?[1]

Now here, in the fourth kind of argument, we really come to action. The classical writers called these questions of *policy*. These arguments answer the question "What should be done about this?"—this situation, this problem, this issue, this difficulty.

So we have defined our bar fight; we now know what caused it; we have determined whether it was a good or bad thing that Joe punched Tom and broke his nose. The question remaining is, what should be done about it? Do we send Joe to prison for four years? Give him a suspended sentence, as it is his first offense? Set him free, and indeed celebrate his courage for standing up to a bully who was threatening others with violence?

Note that I have framed this policy question in three ways—and that each assumes a different answer to the questions associated with the previous three argument types:

- In the first way of framing the policy question (do we send him to prison?), we probably defined the punch (argument type 1) as assault, and maybe worse.
- In the second way (do we give him a suspended sentence?), we might have seen the punch as assault, but in finding out what caused it (argument type 2), we discovered circumstances that led us to think his action was perhaps not all that bad (argument type 3).
- In the third way (do we set him free?), we probably defined the act as self-defense, or even coming to the aid of a threatened innocent (argument type 1); as we discovered that what caused the argument (type 2) was threatening action by the other man, which was really bad (type 3), we decided the punch was not bad at all, but a *good* response, protecting innocent parties (again, type 3).

So what we decide "should be done about it" probably will change as we work our way through the stages of stasis theory. Here again you see the point—and the immense practical value—of stasis theory: to avoid that messy situation where an argument spins out of control because the two sides are talking past each other. With stasis theory, you find the specific place of disagreement so you can then argue productively. Once you and your opponent resolve that moment of stasis, you might move on to the next one, and then the next, until you agree fully. So stasis theory is ultimately an optimistic view on human disagreement: It says that if we can find the precise place where the dispute lies, we can work through that disagreement by means of rational discourse, and both sides can come to see, and act upon, the truth.[2]

And only by working through the first three stages of the argument can we come to a good response and decide on our policy going forward.[3]

Since "policy" is a somewhat abstract term and usually applies to longer-term solutions (as in "we need a policy to deal with sexual harassment in the workplace" or "our foreign policy needs to pivot from the Middle East to dealing with China"), I prefer to call this fourth type of argument a *problem/solution argument*. This terminology helps us see that we might have specific, local problems that do not require a huge "policy"—but it also allows us to consider a crisis in Iraq or Syria, for instance, as one heck of a problem we have on our hands. And we can see right away how, by working through the previous three arguments, we might define the *problem* in very different ways. If the problem is aggressive, violent people threatening others outside a bar, we might see the solution—punching out such types—as a good thing (even if to be used only as a last resort), and what should be done about it is to celebrate such acts of courage in defense of the innocent. But if the problem is that we can't let people respond violently when someone innocently talks to another man's wife, what should be done about it might be to convict and sentence the puncher.

Calling the fourth kind of argument a *problem/solution argument* makes clear the practical side of what we are doing. Even in its title, it points to the tasks that we need to accomplish. (You will see those two tasks shortly, but you can probably guess them right now.)

Let's depart from our bar fight for a while, for problem/solution arguments are around us every day. We have problems in our schools;

we have problems in our economy; we have problems aplenty in our tensions with other nations. We might have problems in our local communities—perhaps the parks are in sorry shape, but we need more businesses to add to the tax base; should we spend tax dollars to refurbish the parks or give a tax break to attract more businesses? Some of the most common kinds of arguments we face, and some of the ones we most immediately need to address, are problem/solution arguments:

- Wolves should be introduced in larger numbers to Yellowstone National Park.
- We need to invest more money in STEM classes and in math education.
- No, we need to get back to the basics of reading, writing, and arithmetic and ignore all these fancy education movements of the moment like STEM.
- Our website is old and clunky and is costing us business; we need to spend the money to completely rework our online presence and include new social media campaigns in our marketing strategies.
- We need to pull back from spending so much on marketing until we have reinvested in our manufacturing capability, because even if we brought in many new customers, we would not be able to produce enough widgets to fill the orders.
- Honey, we need start saving more for the kids' college—they may seem young now, but it's coming sooner than you think!
- Every time I make it to campus I drive around for half an hour trying to find a place to park, and it often makes me late to class. We need to build more parking lots, or even a multistory parking garage.

- Taxes need to be raised on the wealthy so they pay their fair share.
- No, taxes are too high on everyone, and if we overtax the wealthy, they will take their money and their businesses and go elsewhere. We need to reduce taxes.
- This is not a pretty picture in the mirror; I need to get back to the gym![4]

So you see, problem/solution arguments are the lifeblood of politics, economics, business, family life, social life, and even personal life. If we want to move others in the directions we believe our nation, our community, our family, or the team at the office should be taking, we will need to learn how to master problem/solution arguments.

Let's dive right in. What do we need to do to make a successful problem/solution argument?

Shaping the Argument: How to Create Effective Problem/Solution Arguments

If you have made it this far in this book—and I hope, given what I just said about how working through the first three kinds of arguments is important to making good problem/solution arguments, you haven't just skipped to this chapter—you probably don't need a lot of preamble this time. So what do you need to do in this kind of argument?

Just from working through the other chapters and applying what you learned there, you probably have already realized what you need to do, haven't you? If you look at the statements above, you see that there are two parts, or two tasks, implied in those statements:

1. You need to articulate the problem, and
2. You need to lay out and argue for your solution.

That's pretty much it, right? And you know this because you already do it—in your family, with your friends, even with yourself. "Man, I gotta lose some of this weight I built up from Thanksgiving to New Year's [*problem*]. Tomorrow I start cutting the carbs and working out three days a week [*solution*]." "Honey, we are on track to have too little to pay for the kids' college [*problem*]; starting next month we're going to put *x* percent of the paycheck into a college fund [*solution*]."

But to be persuasive in these arguments is another thing entirely, because implementing solutions often means asking people (or yourself) to do something different, something that requires effort or annoyance or expense. Saving for college sounds good, but it means cutting back on eating out, which means planning and cooking dinners every night, cleaning up the dishes, doing more grocery shopping, and so on.

So let's break down these two parts and see how we can be successful in these arguments. To show how this works, I am going to use the one argument that I, in a rare fit of totalitarian behavior, outlaw as a topic in my classes: the lack of parking on campus.[i]

Describing the Problem

As you begin to describe the problem, you will find yourself in one of two situations:

- Everyone with any sense is already aware of the problem, or

i Sorry. Pretty early in my career I had to make this decision; I just couldn't read another paper on the topic. Really. I know I should be more open and patient and student-interest-oriented, but when you grade as many papers as I do, there have to be some limits, if for no other reason than so I can grade everyone *else's* papers with my sanity intact. But I am going to use it as a running example in this chapter, first, because it makes things clear, and second, so I don't inadvertently take on a topic you would like to argue and do your work for you. Oh, and I guess there is a third benefit: By the end of this chapter, you'll be as bored with this topic as I am, and never, ever want to write a paper about it!

- Most people are insufficiently aware of the problem, or perhaps do not know or think there is a problem at all.[5]

If you find yourself in the first situation, this part of your argument is not difficult at all; you simply need to remind your readers of what they already know, perhaps with a few quick facts or details or statistics. If everyone on campus is already grousing about the parking problems, you don't need to persuade them that there is a problem. In fact, belaboring this section of the argument will probably bore and annoy everyone. You do not want your readers thinking, "Yeah, yeah, I know, I know . . . what are you gonna *do* about it?" So in these cases, the first section of your argument will be brief.

But in reality, few problems are actually like this. Even when everyone thinks they know there is a problem, they might define the problem in different terms, or see different causes of the problem, or evaluate the severity of the problem to different degrees.[ii] Think immigration, or climate change, or your family budget, or rescuing the snail darter from extinction—everyone might agree that there is a problem but see it in different lights. In other situations, you might have to introduce your readers to the fact that there is a problem at all. To use a student's example from previous chapters, extroverts might not have any notion that the gregarious, outgoing church structures they have set up might be off-putting to us introverts.[iii] Businessmen making a great deal of money trading with China might not want to think about threats to the world order that

ii I hope you saw what I just did there with the first three kinds of arguments . . .

iii That's the problem with extroverts, right? They're having so much fun being social that they don't realize that we on the introvert side cringe and retreat *because of* the very things they set up to "draw us out." We really don't want someone greeting us at the church door, and we really, really don't want to stand up right before the liturgy begins and shake hands and introduce ourselves to some complete stranger, even if we realize that said stranger is fully loved by God and is our neighbor in the Parable of the Good Samaritan sense of things. We get it, and we really would care for him if he were lying in a ditch, but we cringe at all this engineered sociability, which strikes us as false and contrived. And hear me now: If I have to do one more "icebreaker" activity...

China's aggressive policies and industrial espionage might pose. A spouse might be wonderfully focused on taking care of the many legitimate needs of the cute little toddler in the present and not really be aware of time (and, more important, compound interest) slipping away from the chance to save for college. I knew a man who spent six months in Ethiopia as a missionary, using only a gallon of water for his once-a-week showers, and came back appalled at how much water we waste in America. But how could he persuade his American friends that this waste was a real problem? It is not an easy task when the spigot keeps flowing every time we turn it on.

Notice in all of those examples the importance of knowing, and judging, your readers. For a problem/solution argument, the readership is crucial. There's no point in convincing some random reader that there is problem; you need to persuade those who can actually do something about it—or at least those who can pressure the decision-makers to do something about it. To get your church to change, you probably need to persuade the pastor, or at least a set of people who can go to the pastor and talk him or her into implementing your solution. You can tell your friends and neighbors all you like about the need to save for college, but if your spouse isn't on board, it ain't gonna happen. So when formulating your problem/solution argument, you must determine how to describe the problem based on the needs, positions, and understandings of the more or less specific reader you have in mind.

In most cases, then, your first argumentative task is not just describing the problem but also *persuading your readers that there is a problem*. So what do you do? You draw on the three other kinds of arguments. You might have to define terms and conditions and situations. You often have to make a (quick and effective) causal argument, showing how events, decisions, and conditions in the past have led to (that is, *caused*) the current state of things (that is, the unfortunate *effects*). Ultimately, you need to show that the current situation is, well, *bad*, or at least not so good, or at least not as good as it could be.

Let's take our parking example, showing, along the way, why problem/solution arguments come last in stasis theory:

- *Audience:* Students may be aware of the parking problem, but even they might not know the extent of the problem. Professors may also be aware, but they are not the decision-makers here. Do those campus decision-makers know? Probably not; they might have designated parking spaces next to the administration building and never have to cruise the lots looking for a space. Or administrators might remember a time when fewer students lived off campus and parking was therefore not much of a problem. You will need to describe the problem in a way that will make administrators aware of its severity.
- *Definitional:* Okay, everyone knows what a parking space is, so this might not be a problem here. But perhaps you want to bring up other questions: What is the purpose of a parking lot? Whom does it serve? What is the whole point of having one? And therefore you might find crucial terms that will serve you in defining the problem: convenience, accessibility, safety, etc.
- *Causal:* What is causing the current shortage of parking spaces, and how did we get to this point? Did things change recently in terms of students living off campus and thus needing to drive to class? Was there some other change? What are the effects of the parking crisis? Are students late to class more often? Are they having to park off campus in dodgy areas and having things stolen from their vehicles or even feeling personally unsafe, particularly at night, returning to their cars?

- *Evaluative:* Describing a problem often comes down to showing that the present situation (or perhaps the future if nothing is done in the present) is not good. You might wish to set up criteria: What would be a good, convenient, safe parking situation? By what standards might you judge this? You might look at other campuses and compare them to yours.[6]

Notice once again the role of research, of having extensive evidence (statistics, incidents, historical matter, etc.) on which to draw to persuade your readers of this problem. Unless you are so familiar with the topic that you have all the facts at your fingertips, you will surely have to do some research to help you describe, define, argue causes, and elaborate on the problem.[7] Anecdotal evidence—stories of your difficulty in finding a parking place, for instance—is fine for painting a picture of the problem, but to really persuade others that there is a problem, you must expand from narratives into facts, figures, statistics, and other objective measures. I once had a student who wanted to argue that the rugby club at our school should be elevated to varsity status. His only evidence at the beginning was anecdotal: The rugby club's budget allowed the team to travel to only one out-of-town tournament the previous season. What he needed, I urged, was research to make his points: How small *was* the budget for the rugby club compared to those of other clubs? How many players did this budget serve? What did the rugby club do with that sum, and what could the club *not* do because the sum was so small? How much smaller was the rugby club's budget than the budgets for comparable varsity sports?

Articulating the Solution

Once you have persuaded your readers of the problem, what must you do next? You must articulate your solution. Your readers need to know what you have in mind, and this becomes the thesis of your argument:

- We should get all of our troops out of all Middle Eastern countries, and the sooner the better.
- No, we should reinvest in stability in the Middle East as we did in the 2007 surge and finish the job we started way back in 1991 with the first Gulf War.[8]
- We need to set aside *x* percent of our income and put it into a specific account for a college fund so Junior can attend the school of his choice when he turns eighteen.
- We should set up a special STEM academy in our school district and recruit to it not just the best students but struggling students as well.
- We should dump the expensive STEM programs and reinvest in the classical model of education that has produced more than two thousand years of impressive results in Western culture.
- We need to pause our marketing efforts until we have invested in a complete redesign of our website.
- Rugby should be elevated from a club sport to a varsity sport, enjoying all the privileges and budgetary support of every other varsity sport.
- I should shift to a keto diet, ditch the wasted gym membership, and do those online bodyweight exercises in my apartment every night at 9 p.m.

And finally, just because I can't let go of this one,

- The university should build a six-story parking garage on the footprint of the inadequate parking lot behind the science building.

Your readers are not going to remain patient once you have described the problem; they need to see your solution. (Otherwise, you're just whining, and no one likes that.) Notice that a solution needs clear articulation and, as much as possible, specific action to get the ball rolling. Neither "I need to start losing weight" nor "Something needs to be done about China" is a solution; without a clear plan of action, it is no more than a dreamy, unfocused aspiration.[9]

Arguing for the Solution

Okay, you're done, right? You've laid out the problems and now have told us your solution. Everyone will just fall in line and follow you, right?

You and I both know that's not true. People rarely agree to act just because someone says it is a good idea. And as noted above, solutions rarely are painless—they almost always involve some effort, some sacrifice, some shifting of priorities, some trade-offs. So the only way to convince people to agree to your solution is to show them the real good of your plan of action. To do that, you must accomplish four tasks:[10]

1. You must show that your proposal will solve the problem: You may think that your solution is obvious, but it rarely is. So you will have to walk your readers through how your solution will solve the problem. Chiefly this involves going back through the problems and showing, one by one, how your solution will work to eliminate, or at least mitigate, those problems. And guess what? You are back in causal territory. Now your solution is the cause, and the effects are those you point out. And you will have to take readers through those steps, one by one. How will a six-story structure solve the parking problem on campus? How many spaces will it add? Is that enough? What will be the effects of making rugby a varsity sport? How will that help with the problems the club currently experiences?

2. You must show that your solution is feasible: *Feasible* means, in a sense, "doable." You must show that your organization has the resources to implement your solution—and "resources" include not just financial resources but human resources as well: time, expertise, and motivation. Many solutions that might solve a problem are too expensive, too time-consuming, too politically unreasonable, or just too crazy to be implemented. A student once worried about the invasive zebra mussels that attach themselves to the bottom of boats, and she proposed having an inspector to check every boat as it came out of the water in Texas lakes. I asked whether she had a count of how many lakes there are in Texas, how many boat ramps there are where people take their boats out of the water, and how many staff members would be necessary to cover these ramps 24/7. "Oh," she said. Suddenly she realized what *feasibility* means, and, to her credit, she began thinking of other, more practical solutions to an admittedly real problem on Texas lakes.

Some solutions are not *financially* feasible. To turn to our parking example: To pay for a six-story parking garage, the university might need to increase student fees dramatically. To build up a college fund, a family might need to save 30 percent of its take-home pay—something I doubt many families would find feasible in their monthly budgets. Other solutions might not be *politically* feasible: Would students get angry if the parking garage caused a large increase in their fees? Would professors be up in arms that university funds were being spent on something other than academics or—gasp—professors' potential salary increases? Considering talent and expertise: Does your business have someone on staff who can redesign the website, or will it involve hiring an outside design firm? How much will *that* cost? If there is someone in-house, how will repositioning her time from her current duties affect the business? Even that has a cost, right? How will the rugby team find, and pay for, a now full-time coach? How will it recruit players? Will the increased time and travel commitments of a varsity sport drive away some of the students who enjoy playing it on the club level?[11]

3. You must show that your solution is better than other solutions: This task may sound obvious, but I can't overstate how important it is to accomplish. Solutions are like armpits: Everyone has one—more than one, in fact. If the problem you are discussing is well known, you absolutely can count on the fact that others have already proposed solutions. And even if the problem is unknown, as you describe the problem, *perhaps especially if you do a good job in that section,* your readers are already thinking up solutions.[12] It's just what we do as humans. As I said back in chapter 3, we are cause/effect beings; now we can say it differently: We are problem/solution beings. It's what kept us alive when saber-toothed tigers were ready to eat us if we didn't figure this stuff out.[iv] So you must know about other proposed solutions and how they are supposed to work, what they will cost, and what human resources they will consume. (There's that pesky problem of research again—now you have to research not only your own solution but others' solutions as well. But if you researched the problem, you probably came across those proposed solutions at that point.) And you must show that your solution is better than *all* of those other solutions—perhaps not better in every single metric, but better in the crucial ones (there's that pesky problem of criteria again).

For instance, someone may have proposed using the vast, empty parking lot surrounding the football stadium on campus for overflow parking problems. Why build a parking garage when we can just use that huge lot for parking during the week, especially for those commuter students who show up for just a few hours and then go home? In addressing this solution—which sure seems easy,

iv I know: historically inaccurate, right? But you get the point.

feasible, and readily available—you might show that the stadium's lot is so far away from the academic buildings that students will be incredibly inconvenienced, especially in bad weather, and end up losing valuable academic time getting to and from that parking lot. With regard to the rugby club, someone might argue that seeking better funding for the existing club rather than ramping up to full varsity status might be a better solution. Is there an answer for that argument?

4. Finally, you must deal with any remaining counterarguments against your proposal: By this point, you probably will have covered many counterarguments, but others might remain, both practical and philosophical. Of the latter, I am thinking especially of aesthetic and ethical concerns, neither of which we covered above.[13] Sure, someone might say, a six-story parking garage will add enough spaces, and okay, the university has the budget to do this, but for the love of Pete, parking garages tend to be as ugly as sin, and putting one right behind the science building will wreck the gorgeous campus that is so much a part of our identity here at Ivy-Clad University. We Americans are practical people and tend to make aesthetic considerations secondary, or even tertiary, but they are important. Would you have an answer for that objection? And yes, a colleague might say about a proposal, we could sell many more widgets if we market them in this way, but isn't that deceptive and therefore unethical? A successful problem/solution argument must stand up to these kinds of scrutiny as well, for practical reasons (you could end up in jail) as well as ethical or moral ones (you really do want to do the right thing).

The Problem/Solution Argument Template

As with all of the Four Arguments, I find that it helps to have the tasks laid out in succinct form:

I. Describe the problem
   a. If it is well known, be brief and just remind the reader
   b. If it is not well known, set up the problem:
      i. Define the problem, and/or
      ii. Describe what caused it and its negative effects, and/or
      iii. Show that it is not good by showing how it does not measure up to criteria for this situation/process/activity
II. Articulate your solution
   a. Make it as specific and concrete as possible
   b. Show how it will solve the problem
      i. How it will remove the causes, or lead to good effects
      ii. How it will meet the criteria
   c. Show that the solution is feasible
      i. Do you have the financial resources?
      ii. Do you have the human resources in time and talent?
   d. What incentives does the reader have for implementing this solution?[14]
   e. Show that it is better than other solutions
   f. Deal with any remaining questions/counterarguments
      i. Consider other practical questions
      ii. Consider philosophical questions, especially aesthetic and ethical ones

So once again, you see a two-part argument. The first part might have a varying number of subparts, but the second part definitely has six subparts. Or again, to use the language we have been using, you need to accomplish two tasks to be successful here, and the second task has six subtasks that you will need to accomplish in order to persuade others.

What I have liked from the beginning about stasis theory is this stable sense of *what needs to be accomplished* for each of the Four Arguments. Students are often confused when they move from one teacher to the next because different teachers use different terminology or seem to present writing in different ways. "I thought I learned to write in Professor X's class," a student will plaintively say, "but then the next semester Professor Y wanted something completely different!" But now, I hope you see, it's not a matter of "what Professor X wants" as opposed to "what Professor Y seems to be asking me to do."[v] No, what is important, and what I hope you now see cuts across all argumentative writing, is that each kind of argument involves certain tasks; if you are going to be successful at each kind of argument, you must accomplish these tasks. It's the type and structure of the argument—not the whims of the professor—that set the argument's shape.

v It is always deeply frustrating to us teachers when students come to us with this "I don't know what he wants" kind of complaint, or even more directly asks us, "What do you want in a paper? Because Professor Z wanted something really different, and I was never able to please her." We know Professor X and Professor Y and Professor Z; we know all three of them want a clear thesis, a good argument, and that argument supported by good evidence, the whole thing leading to interesting conclusions, all written in clear, mistake-free prose. Admittedly, professors sometimes contribute to the students' confusion by using different terminology and somewhat different grading rubrics, and by going after these issues in different ways. But some students are too invested in this idea that doing well in classes is a matter of pleasing a professor's tastes and whims. Arguments don't work like that, though. They are not a matter of taste. A good argument does certain things, and a poor one neglects those things.

EXERCISES

Exercise 4.1 Brainstorm some problems. Work with a partner if it helps. Think of problems in your school, your community, your family. Think in different realms—finances, physical space, social issues, relationship issues. Think again of places where you are an expert—here you are likely to be more acutely aware of specific problems and have the expertise to explore them in all their complexity. Think of an industry that captures your attention: solar power, aerospace, the business of classical music, etc. If you are interested, then consider wider problems at the state or national or even international level. Your goal is to come up with a hefty set of problems that you would like to explore.

Here again are some sample theses from my students:

- Because it leads to stress and lost productivity, and no longer provides any real benefits, we should eliminate Daylight Savings Time.[15]
- Churches should do more to cater to the needs of introverted members by offering alternative, quieter services, more one-on-one interactions, and perhaps online features, dialing back the loud, forced sociability of so many of their activities.[vi]
- For lawns in the southwestern United States, we should promote the use of native grasses, as they save water and pesticide runoff and foster healthier communities.[16]
- College students should call their moms once a week.
- To combat colony collapse disorder and to preserve

vi I wanted to include this to show you how the student progressed in thinking about this topic of churches and introverts, and how, by the end of the semester, she had fully used stasis theory to work from a more general, unfocused definitional argument all the way to a concrete, specific problem/solution argument.

honeybee populations, strict limits should be placed on the amount of pesticide farmers can spray on a weekly basis.[17]

- Though it will be costly, we should hire a biweekly house cleaner so we can have more time with the children.
- Everyone in the family should follow my efficient method for loading the dishwasher.[vii]
- Schools should require music, arts, and athletics from all their students every year because the health of the body and the harmoniousness of the eye and the ear are as important as the growth of the intellect.

Exercise 4.2 Using the template (see pages 113–114), map out how you will present your problem/solution argument:

- Consider how well known your problem is and how much you will have to convince your reader that there is a problem, or how severe it is, or how bad the consequences are of not addressing the problem.
- Consider whether you will use definitional, causal, or evaluative means to describe the problem.
- Articulate a solution that is clear and specific.
- Consider how you will show that your solution will solve the problem. What evidence will you use? Will you use causal methods?
- Using your research, show that your solution is feasible—that you have the financial and human resources to implement your solution.
- Show that your solution is better than other solutions.

---

vii A student wrote this argument, but I had to ask her, “Have you been talking to my family?” And I had to admit that “feasibility” in terms of human resources is a huge problem here: I struggled to see three-dimensional spaces as well as did others in my house, so achieving the competence to implement this solution is an uphill battle!

- End by dealing with any remaining counterarguments to your solution.

Work through these questions and begin organizing your argument according to the template.

Exercise 4.3 When you are ready, write up your argument, focusing on accomplishing the tasks step by step. Offer your readers a good introductory description of the problem, and then lead them through your solution and why it is a good one, one section at a time. Always consider other solutions and counterarguments to your proposal, and consider how you will motivate your readers to take on the additional work, or annoyance, or make the changes that will bring about your solution.

Incentives? Why Incentives?[18]

You may have noticed that I slipped into the template a line that I have not yet discussed: "What incentives does your reader have for implementing this solution?" I deliberately set that aside above, but now I want to explain the origin of that part of the template.

When I teach problem/solution arguments, I am sometimes surprised at the way students propose their solutions; they seem to think that just because something is good and true and right, people will automatically want to respond. The student arguing to make rugby a varsity sport did not consider that the change would involve significant expense. He just saw all the good that would come from making rugby a varsity sport and thought that would carry the argument. I had to ask, "Where is the money going to come from? And if no new money is coming in, what incentive does the athletic director have for dividing up his limited budget to provide for a new team?" In another case, an earnest, thoughtful Catholic student once proposed that, to reduce abortions, every abortion doctor should show an ultrasound of the baby in utero to every woman who comes to the clinic. "Why would an abortion doctor do that?" I asked her. "Well," she said, "because it's the right thing to do." Hmm, I responded: "Does he have any economic incentive, or any other kind, to show pregnant women a live picture of their babies in their wombs?" She paused, not quite sure how to answer. "So, if he doesn't, how are you going to *make* him?"

Many other students proposed solutions that were similarly impractical, that did not pass the feasibility test. That is why I added this line to the template: *You need to show what incentives there are for your readers to act on your proposal.* How can you incentivize the government to get rid of Daylight Savings Time? How can you encourage those lazy, good-for-nothing family members of yours to load the dishwasher the right way? It may be nice to preach about changing people's lawns in the Southwest, but in what ways are you going to make it easy and inexpensive for them to pull up all that Bermuda grass and put in native grasses?

But the students' idea that people should do things "just because it's the right thing to do" persisted. It was almost as if offering incentives seemed tawdry to them—I shouldn't need to incentivize this, they sometimes said; people should do things because they are right! So I began to wonder whether there might be a theological explanation: The students needed to be reminded of the fundamental Judeo-Christian notion of fallenness. That is, my students—most of them Catholic, almost all of them Christian in one way or another—needed to be reminded that, since the Garden of Eden and the acts of what Ishmael in *Moby-Dick* calls "the two orchard thieves," something has been fundamentally broken in human nature, and that makes it difficult for us to do what is true and good just because it's true and good. The students had an optimistic attitude toward human nature, believing that humans will strive for the good simply because you set it in front of them. But experience tells us that this sadly is not so, and that people often work from self-regarding, if not selfish, motives. Or maybe it's just what I said above: Implementing solutions, even ones you think are necessary and important, involves effort, change, annoyance, even pain.

The great historian John Lukacs, a Catholic, once said that it might be more important, or at least more essential, to first persuade people of the Fall than of the rest of the Christian message. I am beginning to think Lukacs was right: If someone does not undeceive us about our fallenness, we tend to have a dangerously optimistic view of human nature. In my own college days, I wanted so badly for everyone to be good, to do the good. I used to think plaintively that doing the good was simply a matter of being taught the right things, brought up well, and put in the right environments. But the conflict and strife I saw all around, I realized, were not simply problems of educational and social engineering—and that I was a part of that problem myself.

Sometimes an optimistic view of human nature is sweetly naïve and easily corrected. After I nudged my student to consider why an abortionist would voluntarily show a pregnant woman an ultrasound of her baby, the student sheepishly conceded this naïveté and reworked her argument. Similarly, the student making the argument about rugby realized he needed to do more research on the costs and budgets of varsity sports, and he began to add in other arguments—for instance, that having a rugby team would help the admissions office recruit more male students, a definite need when women now outnumber men on many campuses.

But a more deeply entrenched opposition to the lessons of the Fall can be more troubling. If we think that people should be good, and that the way to get them there is to engineer education and social structures in the right way, we can succumb to utopian thinking that suggests people *should just do what we think they should do because we are sure it is good for them, whether they see it or not.*

But of course people are not universally good, and even those who are good are not good all the time. We are all products of the Fall: broken, divided against ourselves, as Augustine says, knowing what is good and doing the opposite anyway. (When I finally understood this, I became, oddly enough, happier, more content in the world, and more accepting of my fellow man.) But the utopian man, frustrated, begins to use coercive measures to *force* people to choose the good he is convinced is so simple and obvious, if only these recalcitrant idiots would just do what is right and good! And that is how we end up with the gulags in Soviet Russia and reeducation camps in Pol Pot's Cambodia, and how regimes end up, with an apparently clear conscience, "eliminating" those who, despite the regime's "well-meaning" efforts to get them in line, resist doing so.

The alternative, then, is prudence, which is the virtue of choosing the practical good insofar as it can be achieved in the given circumstance. Prudence accepts that there are limits to what we can do in this space and time. Prudence accepts that people are fallen, that they *can* act toward the good but often struggle to do so. Prudence accepts that we must protect ourselves against the weaker and more troubling side of people's fallen nature—and our own as well. So prudence accepts with a certain humility that I might not have all the answers to every problem right now, and that I might want to listen to others who are thinking about these issues. Prudence is tough; it's a virtue that takes patience, experience, endurance, and perceptiveness. I cannot say I have fully mastered it myself. And when we propose solutions, we cannot count on our readers to possess a deeply ingrained virtue of prudence, either. But we appeal to their better angels, and offer those angels incentives for moving toward the good, all the while realizing that their fallenness—and our own—is there, and part of the struggle.

That is what we do when we argue: As Aristotle noted, we are engaged in the process of soul-leading. A healthy optimism is a part of every attempt to argue. But it should be an optimism infused with hard-won prudence, with a recognition of fallenness that makes us realize the struggle involved in leading other souls, *and our own*, to the good, the true, and the beautiful. Such struggle should remind us that we won't perfectly solve all the world's problems; that wonderful paradise will come only at the end of time, and is not our business.

EXTRA FUN WITH PROBLEM/SOLUTION ARGUMENTS

A Classic Problem/Solution Argument
Jonathan Swift's "A Modest Proposal"[19]

The greatest, or at least the most fun, problem/solution argument of all time, Jonathan Swift's essay "A Modest Proposal," was a response to terrible conditions in Ireland in the eighteenth century. Swift felt that the policies of the British government had caused, or at least exacerbated, poverty in Ireland. He published "A Modest Proposal" in 1729 in response to various proposed solutions he thought likely to be ineffective in dealing with Ireland's problems.

This essay is longer than the classic Shakespearean texts I featured at the end of the other chapters. But I include it in full here so you can see how Swift sets out the problem and then argues for his (rather unusual!) solution. Pay particular attention to how he uses the various tasks of the problem/solution argument to create the effects he wants to create.[20] Notice the care he devotes to exploring the feasibility of his solution. He even suggests how his solution is better than all the other solutions.

After you read it, discuss with your classmates how Swift is working here. What is the basis for his anger? How does he channel that anger into this very unusual argument? Where do you see Swift articulating his *real* solutions?

A MODEST PROPOSAL

For preventing the children of poor people in Ireland, from being a burden on their parents or country, and for making them beneficial to the publick.

by Jonathan Swift

It is a melancholy object to those, who walk through this great town, or travel in the country, when they see the streets, the roads, and cabin-doors crowded with beggars of the female sex, followed by three, four, or six children, all in rags, and importuning every passenger for an alms. These mothers, instead of being able to work for their honest livelihood, are forced to employ all their time in strolling to beg sustenance for their helpless infants who, as they grow up, either turn thieves for want of work, or leave their dear native country, to fight for the Pretender in Spain, or sell themselves to the Barbadoes.

I think it is agreed by all parties, that this prodigious number of children in the arms, or on the backs, or at the heels of their mothers, and frequently of their fathers, is in the present deplorable state of the kingdom, a very great additional grievance; and therefore whoever could find out a fair, cheap and easy method of making these children sound and useful members of the commonwealth, would deserve so well of the publick, as to have his statue set up for a preserver of the nation.

But my intention is very far from being confined to provide only for the children of professed beggars: it is of a much greater extent, and shall take in the whole number of infants at a certain age, who are born of parents in effect as little able to support them, as those who demand our charity in the streets.

As to my own part, having turned my thoughts for many years upon this important subject, and maturely weighed the several schemes of our projectors, I have always found them grossly mistaken in their computation. It is true, a child just dropt from its dam, may be supported by her milk, for a solar year, with little other nourishment: at most not above the value of two shillings, which the mother may certainly get, or the value in scraps, by her lawful occupation of begging; and it is exactly at one year old that I propose to provide for them in such a manner, as, instead of being a charge upon their parents, or the parish, or wanting food and raiment for the rest of their lives, they shall, on the contrary, contribute to the feeding, and partly to the clothing of many thousands.

There is likewise another great advantage in my scheme, that it will prevent those voluntary abortions, and that horrid practice of women murdering their bastard children, alas! too frequent among us, sacrificing the poor innocent babes, I doubt, more to avoid the expence than the shame, which would move tears and pity in the most savage and inhuman breast.

The number of souls in this kingdom being usually reckoned one million and a half, of these I calculate there may be about two hundred thousand couple, whose wives are breeders; from which number I subtract thirty thousand couple, who are able to maintain their own children, (although I apprehend there cannot be so many under the present distresses of the kingdom) but this being granted, there will remain a hundred and seventy thousand breeders. I again subtract fifty thousand, for those women who miscarry, or whose children die by accident or disease within the year. There only remain a hundred and twenty thousand children of poor parents annually born. The question therefore is, How this number shall be reared and provided for? which, as I have already said, under the present situation of affairs, is utterly impossible by all the methods hitherto proposed. For we can neither employ them in handicraft or agriculture; they neither build houses, (I mean in the country) nor cultivate land: they can very seldom pick up a livelihood by stealing till they arrive at six years old; except where they are of towardly parts, although I confess they learn the rudiments much earlier; during which time they can however be properly looked upon only as probationers; as I have been informed by a principal gentleman in the county of Cavan, who protested to me, that he never knew above one or two instances under the age of six, even in a part of the kingdom so renowned for the quickest proficiency in that art.

I am assured by our merchants, that a boy or a girl, before twelve years old, is no saleable commodity, and even when they come to this age, they will not yield above three pounds, or three pounds and half a crown at most, on the exchange; which cannot turn to account either to the parents or kingdom, the charge of nutriments and rags having been at least four times that value.

I shall now therefore humbly propose my own thoughts, which I hope will not be liable to the least objection.

I have been assured by a very knowing American of my acquaintance in London, that a young healthy child well nursed, is, at a year old, a most delicious nourishing and wholesome food, whether stewed, roasted, baked, or boiled; and I make no doubt that it will equally serve in a fricasee, or a ragout.

I do therefore humbly offer it to publick consideration, that of the hundred and twenty thousand children, already computed, twenty thousand may be reserved for breed, whereof only one fourth part to be males; which is more than we allow to sheep, black cattle, or swine, and my reason is, that these children are seldom the fruits of marriage, a circumstance not much regarded by our savages, therefore, one male will be sufficient to serve four females. That the remaining hundred thousand may, at a year old, be offered in sale to the persons of quality and fortune, through the kingdom, always advising the mother to let them suck plentifully in the last month, so as to render them plump, and fat for a good table. A child will make two dishes at an entertainment for friends, and when the family dines alone, the fore or hind quarter will make a reasonable dish, and seasoned with a little pepper or salt, will be very good boiled on the fourth day, especially in winter.

I have reckoned upon a medium, that a child just born will weigh 12 pounds, and in a solar year, if tolerably nursed, encreaseth to 28 pounds.

I grant this food will be somewhat dear, and therefore very proper for landlords, who, as they have already devoured most of the parents, seem to have the best title to the children.

Infant's flesh will be in season throughout the year, but more plentiful in March, and a little before and after; for we are told by a grave author, an eminent French physician, that fish being a prolifick dyet, there are more children born in Roman Catholick countries about nine months after Lent, than at any other season; therefore, reckoning a year after Lent, the markets will be more glutted than usual, because the number of Popish infants, is at least three to one in this kingdom, and therefore it will have one other collateral advantage, by lessening the number of Papists among us.

I have already computed the charge of nursing a beggar's child (in which list I reckon all cottagers, labourers, and four-fifths of the farmers) to be about two shillings per annum, rags included; and I believe no gentleman would repine to give ten shillings for the carcass of a good fat child, which, as I have said, will make four dishes of excellent nutritive meat, when he hath only some particular friend, or his own family to dine with him. Thus the squire will learn to be a good landlord, and grow popular among his tenants, the mother will have eight shillings neat profit, and be fit for work till she produces another child.

Those who are more thrifty (as I must confess the times require) may flay the carcass; the skin of which, artificially dressed, will make admirable gloves for ladies, and summer boots for fine gentlemen.

As to our City of Dublin, shambles may be appointed for this purpose, in the most convenient parts of it, and butchers we may be assured will not be wanting; although I rather recommend buying the children alive, and dressing them hot from the knife, as we do roasting pigs.

A very worthy person, a true lover of his country, and whose virtues I highly esteem, was lately pleased in discoursing on this matter, to offer a refinement upon my scheme. He said, that many gentlemen of this kingdom, having of late destroyed their deer, he conceived that the want of venison might be well supplied by the bodies of young lads and maidens, not exceeding fourteen years of age, nor under twelve; so great a number of both sexes in every county being now ready to starve for want of work and service: and these to be disposed of by their parents if alive, or otherwise by their nearest relations. But with due deference to so excellent a friend, and so deserving a patriot, I cannot be altogether in his sentiments; for as to the males, my American acquaintance assured me from frequent experience, that their flesh was generally tough and lean, like that of our schoolboys, by continual exercise, and their taste disagreeable, and to fatten them would not answer the charge. Then as to the females, it would, I think, with humble submission, be a loss to the publick, because they soon would become breeders themselves: and besides, it is not improbable that some scrupulous people might be apt to censure such a practice, (although indeed very unjustly) as a little bordering upon cruelty, which, I confess, hath always been with me the strongest objection against any project, how well soever intended.

But in order to justify my friend, he confessed, that this expedient was put into his head by the famous Psalmanaazor, a native of the island Formosa, who came from thence to London, above twenty years ago, and in conversation told my friend, that in his country, when any young person happened to be put to death, the executioner sold the carcass to persons of quality, as a prime dainty; and that, in his time, the body of a plump girl of fifteen, who was crucified for an attempt to poison the Emperor, was sold to his imperial majesty's prime minister of state, and other great mandarins of the court in joints from the gibbet, at four hundred crowns. Neither indeed can I deny, that if the same use were made of several plump young girls in this town, who without one single groat to their fortunes, cannot stir abroad without a chair, and appear at a playhouse and assemblies in foreign fineries which they never will pay for, the kingdom would not be the worse.

Some persons of a desponding spirit are in great concern about that vast number of poor people, who are aged, diseased, or maimed; and I have been desired to employ my thoughts what course may be taken, to ease the nation of so grievous an incumbrance. But I am not in the least pain upon that matter, because it is very well known, that they are every day dying, and rotting, by cold and famine, and filth, and vermin, as fast as can be reasonably expected. And as to the young labourers, they are now in almost as hopeful a condition. They cannot get work, and consequently pine away from want of nourishment, to a degree, that if at any time they are accidentally hired to common labour, they have not strength to perform it, and thus the country and themselves are happily delivered from the evils to come.

I have too long digressed, and therefore shall return to my subject. I think the advantages by the proposal which I have made are obvious and many, as well as of the highest importance.

For first, as I have already observed, it would greatly lessen the number of Papists, with whom we are yearly overrun, being the principal breeders of the nation, as well as our most dangerous enemies, and who stay at home on purpose with a design to deliver the kingdom to the Pretender, hoping to take their advantage by the absence of so many good Protestants, who have chosen rather to leave their country, than stay at home and pay tithes against their conscience to an episcopal curate.

Secondly, The poorer tenants will have something valuable of their own, which by law may be made liable to a distress, and help to pay their landlord's rent, their corn and cattle being already seized, and money a thing unknown.

Thirdly, Whereas the maintenance of a hundred thousand children, from two years old, and upwards, cannot be computed at less than ten shillings a piece per annum, the nation's stock will be thereby encreased fifty thousand pounds per annum, besides the profit of a new dish, introduced to the tables of all gentlemen of fortune in the kingdom, who have any refinement in taste. And the money will circulate among our selves, the goods being entirely of our own growth and manufacture.

Fourthly, The constant breeders, besides the gain of eight shillings sterling per annum by the sale of their children, will be rid of the charge of maintaining them after the first year.

Fifthly, This food would likewise bring great custom to taverns, where the vintners will certainly be so prudent as to procure the best receipts for dressing it to perfection; and consequently have their houses frequented by all the fine gentlemen, who justly value themselves upon their knowledge in good eating; and a skilful cook, who understands how to oblige his guests, will contrive to make it as expensive as they please.

Sixthly, This would be a great inducement to marriage, which all wise nations have either encouraged by rewards, or enforced by laws and penalties. It would encrease the care and tenderness of mothers towards their children, when they were sure of a settlement for life to the poor babes, provided in some sort by the publick, to their annual profit instead of expence. We should soon see an honest emulation among the married women, which of them could bring the fattest child to the market. Men would become as fond of their wives, during the time of their pregnancy, as they are now of their mares in foal, their cows in calf, or sows when they are ready to farrow; nor offer to beat or kick them (as is too frequent a practice) for fear of a miscarriage.

Many other advantages might be enumerated. For instance, the addition of some thousand carcasses in our exportation of barrel'd beef: the propagation of swine's flesh, and improvement in the art of making good bacon, so much wanted among us by the great destruction of pigs, too frequent at our tables; which are no way comparable in taste or magnificence to a well grown, fat yearling child, which roasted whole will make a considerable figure at a Lord Mayor's feast, or any other publick entertainment. But this, and many others, I omit, being studious of brevity.

Supposing that one thousand families in this city, would be constant customers for infants flesh, besides others who might have it at merry meetings, particularly at weddings and christenings, I compute that Dublin would take off annually about twenty thousand carcasses; and the rest of the kingdom (where probably they will be sold somewhat cheaper) the remaining eighty thousand.

I can think of no one objection, that will possibly be raised against this proposal, unless it should be urged, that the number of people will be thereby much lessened in the kingdom. This I freely own, and was indeed one principal design in offering it to the world. I desire the reader will observe, that I calculate my remedy for this one individual Kingdom of Ireland, and for no other that ever was, is, or, I think, ever can be upon Earth. Therefore let no man talk to me of other expedients: Of taxing our absentees at five shillings a pound: Of using neither clothes, nor houshold furniture, except what is of our own growth and manufacture: Of utterly rejecting the materials and instruments that promote foreign luxury: Of curing the expensiveness of pride, vanity, idleness, and gaming in our women: Of introducing a vein of parsimony, prudence and temperance: Of learning to love our country, wherein we differ even from Laplanders, and the inhabitants of Topinamboo: Of quitting our animosities and factions, nor acting any longer like the Jews, who were murdering one another at the very moment their city was taken: Of being a little cautious not to sell our country and consciences for nothing: Of teaching landlords to have at least one degree of mercy towards their tenants. Lastly, of putting a spirit of honesty, industry, and skill into our shopkeepers, who, if a resolution could now be taken to buy only our native goods, would immediately unite to cheat and exact upon us in the price, the measure, and the goodness, nor could ever yet be brought to make one fair proposal of just dealing, though often and earnestly invited to it.

Therefore I repeat, let no man talk to me of these and the like expedients, till he hath at least some glympse of hope, that there will ever be some hearty and sincere attempt to put them into practice.

But, as to myself, having been wearied out for many years with offering vain, idle, visionary thoughts, and at length utterly despairing of success, I fortunately fell upon this proposal, which, as it is wholly new, so it hath something solid and real, of no expence and little trouble, full in our own power, and whereby we can incur no danger in disobliging England. For this kind of commodity will not bear exportation, and flesh being of too tender a consistence, to admit a long continuance in salt, although perhaps I could name a country, which would be glad to eat up our whole nation without it.

After all, I am not so violently bent upon my own opinion, as to reject any offer, proposed by wise men, which shall be found equally innocent, cheap, easy, and effectual. But before something of that kind shall be advanced in contradiction to my scheme, and offering a better, I desire the author or authors will be pleased maturely to consider two points. First, As things now stand, how they will be able to find food and raiment for a hundred thousand useless mouths and backs. And secondly, There being a round million of creatures in humane figure throughout this kingdom, whose whole subsistence put into a common stock, would leave them in debt two million of pounds sterling, adding those who are beggars by profession, to the bulk of farmers, cottagers and labourers, with their wives and children, who are beggars in effect; I desire those politicians who dislike my overture, and may perhaps be so bold to attempt an answer, that they will first ask the parents of these mortals, whether they would not at this day think it a great happiness to have been sold for food at a year old, in the manner I prescribe, and thereby have avoided such a perpetual scene of misfortunes, as they have since gone through, by the oppression of landlords, the impossibility of paying rent without money or trade, the want of common sustenance, with neither house nor clothes to cover them from the inclemencies of the weather, and the most inevitable prospect of intailing the like, or greater miseries, upon their breed for ever.

I profess in the sincerity of my heart, that I have not the least personal interest in endeavouring to promote this necessary work, having no other motive than the publick good of my country, by advancing our trade, providing for infants, relieving the poor, and giving some pleasure to the rich. I have no children, by which I can propose to get a single penny; the youngest being nine years old, and my wife past child-bearing.

CHAPTER FIVE

ARGUING IN DIFFERENT DISCIPLINES

or

ARGUMENTS ACROSS THE CURRICULUM

We have seen how stasis theory takes us through an issue, showing us where the point of contention is and thus where we need to begin our argument. And we have seen how to build each of the Four Arguments. We also have templates for building each of those kinds of arguments. And now that we know how each of these arguments work—what tasks they must accomplish—we have rubrics for analyzing others' arguments, measuring whether they have completed these tasks successfully.

How can this help you in the real world of your classes, and later your career writing papers or preparing a presentation for your clients?[1] I want to explore with you some of the ways that learning stasis theory and the Four Arguments can be useful in these endeavors, and then I want to explore in detail my own field—literature analysis—as a special test case. I once thought that stasis theory had nothing to do with my work teaching literature, but it turned out to be extremely effective in teaching students how to write papers. If you can use stasis theory there, you can use it anywhere.

How Different Disciplines Argue

The first title of this chapter is "Arguing in Different Disciplines." I chose that title because I was taught as an undergraduate to call majors or fields of study "disciplines," and I have liked that language ever since. Note the double meaning: to learn a discipline, you must *discipline yourself.* That is, you must submit to the ways of thinking that characterize that subject. To think like an economist, a biologist, or a literary critic means learning the discipline of that field—its characteristic concepts, ideas, vocabulary, and intellectual models. To learn a discipline, to fully enter into it as a way of thinking, takes hard work: You have to buckle down, do the problem sets or the reading, learn the concepts, and master the material in a way that it becomes second nature. This is why in the Renaissance, a painter's apprentice started by sweeping the floors, then moved to mixing pigments, then eventually was allowed to craft practice pieces, then perhaps did some simple fill-in work for the master, and through that long process developed into a painter himself. He had to discipline his head and hands and imagination to master his art.[i] Similarly, when you hire a lawyer, you don't want one who is still learning cases and precedents; you want one who has worked so hard to discipline herself by learning all of the relevant cases that she automatically thinks in the terms of her discipline. Early in college, I studied biochemistry and learned to think in terms of the way enzymes interact with other chemicals, largely in cause/effect relationships. But I changed my major to English, went off to graduate school to become a professional in that discipline, and now I think in terms of metaphor, image, and

i In *The Writer's Workshop*, my first book, I explored this notion of the Renaissance painter's apprenticeship to show how imitation is one of the surest ways to develop your knowledge in a discipline, how imitating the greats is the way humans have always learned complex subjects, and how imitation can help you become a better writer.

narrative. When I hear a politician's speech, I think about the metaphors he uses, the images his ads deploy, and the narratives he builds around his campaign. I have *disciplined* myself to learn that *discipline* of literary and rhetorical thinking, and it is deeply embedded in my thought; by disciplining myself I have learned a new way of thinking that now feels instinctual. In Aristotelian terms, it has become a habit.[2]

This book walks you through the first steps in learning the discipline of—and disciplining yourself to learn—rhetoric, the art of argument. If you discipline yourself to learn the structures of arguments, if you know the four templates so well that you internalize them, then you will start to see these arguments all around you and naturally begin to evaluate whether they are persuasive or not. And when you find yourself needing to build an argument, you will much more easily see the tasks you need to accomplish to be successful. Few things make me happier than when a former student comes to me and says, "I was working on a paper the other day, and realized all I needed to do was to stack a definitional argument on top of my evaluative argument, and soon the paper's structure was obvious and easy." You will be able to do this in whatever field—whatever discipline—you choose to study.

Thus the second title of this chapter, "Arguments Across the Curriculum," suggests that in whatever field you study, whether it is history, biology, economics, or physical therapy, you are going to deal with arguments. Throughout this book I have used examples from different fields—and encouraged you to brainstorm ideas from your own interests—to demonstrate this in action. But I want to make it explicit: Every field has its controversies, and therefore in every field people make arguments. "Even science?" some of you might be thinking. "We just study the facts of nature; we don't make arguments." But *of course* scientists argue! Copernicus had to *argue for* the heliocentric universe, and then Galileo added more evidence and took the argument even further.[ii] Einstein wrote a series of papers *arguing for* his theory of relativity, and he won the argument even before there was experimental evidence to prove it conclusively. That's what a scientific paper is: an *argument* showing that the experiments you conducted, the ideas and models you are putting forward, explain something about nature that no one has described before.[3]

You will need to master the Four Arguments in order to be successful in any field, and you will need to know which kinds of arguments your chosen discipline tends to make. And after college, when you are a professional working in that field, you will make continue to make arguments, with even higher stakes.

Let's explore the ways some of the major disciplines argue:[4]

- Take history, for instance. We have already discussed how historians deal largely, you might say exclusively, in causes and effects. How did something happen? What led ancient Rome to change from a republic to an empire? How did the ancient Greek theater get started: What were its antecedents, and how did they lead to the great flowering of Greek drama in the fifth century B.C.? What were the causes of the Great Depression, and what happened as a result? What happened to the Whig Party, why did it collapse, and how did something else come along to take its place?

---

ii Interestingly, Galileo made his argument in the form of a dialogue, and he gave the losing argument to a cardinal in the Catholic Church who disagreed with him. In making the cardinal look stupid, Galileo gained a powerful enemy, and it was this as much as anything that got him in trouble. The pope at the time had been a big supporter of all of Galileo's work and had no problem with the Copernican heliocentric view of the universe. But even the pope couldn't save Galileo from this enraged cardinal, and so the scientist was sentenced to a (rather mild) house arrest in a beautiful villa on the edge of Rome. Perhaps one lesson here is to be careful when you argue not to make your opponents look stupid; treat them with charity, even if you think they are dead wrong, not just because they might avenge their hurt upon you but because it is the right thing to do. They probably came to their positions through their own thoughts and experiences; you should respect that and treat them accordingly.

- All of the natural sciences, as you can see above, also deal in causes and effects. As we noted when we talked about Aristotle's four causes, the natural sciences are interested in the formal and efficient cause: What is this made of, and how does this work? In the 1940s and 1950s, the great question that James Watson, Francis Crick, and Maurice Wilkins (and, we now know, Rosalind Franklin) solved with their work on modeling DNA was, how does the genetics Gregor Mendel described really work on the molecular level?
- The social sciences, of course, borrow their methods from the natural sciences. Economics, for instance, studies the law of supply and demand, which describes markets and prices in much the same way that physical laws describe heat or tension or cells. Political scientists define systems of government, study how those systems create varying effects, and evaluate the worth of those systems to guide decisions for the future. They also track polls to understand, and predict, how elections work.
- In business, as we have seen from previous examples, all four arguments are taking place all the time. Businessmen and women need knowledge of macroeconomic causes and effects: How is a change in European markets or monetary policy going to change trade with American firms? Marketing departments define a product, research the effects different marketing campaigns have had on similar products, and evaluate the effectiveness of marketing strategies. Accountants deal in definitions all the time: What kind of cost is this? How do we separate out these various kinds of expenses? They also study causes and effects of models of revenue and spending. And ultimately, businessmen and women are interested in solving problems and producing solutions: What is

the best way to reach new customers, expand into a new market, or acquire a new product line?

- Philosophers and theologians engage in all four kinds of arguments. What is the good, the true, and the beautiful? Socrates walked around Athens asking people all sorts of questions, and he discovered that none of them really knew how to define justice, happiness, or law. How would you make the ideal city, if you could build it from scratch? What problems would you try to solve? In the *Poetics*, Aristotle asks, what is tragedy (definitional), what parts does it have and which parts are more important than others (evaluative), and how can you tell if a play is well made (evaluative)? You might even say that Aristotle asked, what problems does the *polis* solve by having a functioning theater (problem/solution)? Many philosophers have taken up the questions of whether the universe has always existed or whether it can be shown that it had a beginning. They evaluate things: What is the best political system for true human flourishing? In fact, they are better than all of the other disciplines at asking about final causes: What are human beings *for*? What is a church, what is its purpose, how can you tell a healthy one from a weak one, and how can you deal with problems in it? Can you prove the existence of God? What (or Who) is God, anyway? Science cannot answer these questions—it is not designed to answer these questions; it excludes them. So they must be addressed by philosophers and theologians—and all of us. As a professor once told me, "Everyone is religious, in that everyone, at some point in his or her life, asks the question, 'What does it all mean? What is the purpose of life?'" That's why we need philosophers and theologians to fully explore the Four Arguments—and pursue the truth about our existence.

Using the Four Arguments in Real Life

At the beginning of this book, I gave you a quiz called "What Kind of Argument Am I?" I hope that when you revisit that test, it will seem much easier to you; you have learned how to recognize the different kinds of arguments and can use this information "out in the wild."[5] When you are in a class, reading an essay assignment, or attending a business meeting, you will be able to recognize what kind of argument is being made—or you are being asked to make—and, with your knowledge of the arguments' templates, you will know which tasks that kind of argument must accomplish, and in which order. And you will now be able to judge how successful those arguments are by asking whether they complete those tasks.

In real life, people often layer different arguments over one another in complex ways. Sure, there are many times, when you deal with one of the four kinds of arguments in isolation. But there are other times when you find yourself combining two or more of them. Recall the student mentioned above who developed a definitional argument as preliminary to his causal argument. Or remember how, in a problem/solution argument, you might have to describe the problem by showing the causes and deleterious effects of the problem before moving on to the solution.

Indeed, many of the real-world problems you will address throughout your life will be of this nature, requiring you to combine two or more of the Four Arguments. That is all the more reason for you to master them now, in isolation. Mastering—and I mean really mastering—the templates of the Four Arguments is important so you can later use them together in these complex ways. Think of mastering the Four Arguments as like doing practice drills in a sport so you can combine those skills on the court when the game is whizzing around you. Or think of it like music, where you need to practice your scales and arpeggios so you can play the music that uses those scales and arpeggios in fascinating ways. If you master the structures of the Four Arguments, you will be like a jazz musician who has memorized every one of the major and minor scales, the blues scales and the pentatonic scales, so that when he improvises, they are simply there, ready for him to draw upon them as easily as moving his fingers to play a B-flat note. Once you master the four templates in this way—the four scales or arpeggios, the dribbling and passing skills of arguing—you will develop, organize, and execute your persuasive writing with ease.

A Test Case—Literary Criticism

Let us see together whether, and if so how, stasis theory can help us with the complex art of explicating literary texts. Most of you will, at some point or another, take a course that involves reading and analyzing literature; later on, you will continue to read novels, see films and other dramas, maybe even read some poems—and talk about them with your friends. I am constantly watching and listening to young people, now that the three trilogies are complete, arguing about *Star Wars*—which is the best, why the first trilogy is so bad, whether the final trilogy lives up to the promise of the original films, and more. These arguments are actually engaging in film criticism, which I think of as a subset of literary criticism.

For a long time, I didn't teach stasis theory in my literature classes. I had used it in my composition and rhetoric classes at Northwest Missouri State University, but when I began teaching in the Great Books Core Curriculum at the University of Dallas, stasis theory didn't seem relevant to my course assignments. I'm not asking them to *define* a lyric poem, right? And I'm not asking them to write about what *caused* the *Iliad* or the *Divine Comedy*, I thought. Nor was I asking them to *evaluate* whether *Paradise*

Lost is a great work; we assumed that as a precondition for studying it. And besides, evaluations are the province of book reviewers; I wasn't asking them to write a review of the *Aeneid*. And I definitely wasn't asking them to *solve problems*—as if the point of reading *Beowulf* was to make it "relevant" by applying it to some real-world issue. (That would mean turning the text into some Aesop's fable with a tidy moral; I strenuously resist when people do that with great literature because it robs it of its richness and nuance.) No, I was asking them to *interpret* the text, to draw out its meaning and convey it to others. That didn't fit in any of the Four Arguments, it seemed to me.

But then I was left with a problem. Is there something wrong with stasis theory? Does it leave out an important kind of argument, the *interpretive argument* that I was teaching in my literature classes? If this kind of argument doesn't fit in the scheme—and this is where I began to be really perplexed—what on earth *is* an interpretive argument? What is the question it is asking and what are the tasks it needs to accomplish to be successful? Is it a fifth type of argument? Or was I missing something that would show me how interpretive arguments fit into the four-argument scheme? If literary interpretation did fit the scheme, how?[6]

To solve my puzzle, I turned to my colleagues who teach literature and writing. I asked for the prompts they use for their students' papers in order to see what interpretive arguments they were asking their students to make. What I got back surprised me: Stasis theory was there, hiding in plain sight.

Take, for instance, this paper prompt on the *Iliad* from my now-retired colleague Dr. Eileen Gregory, renowned and beloved for her attention to her students' work. The prompt refers to the moving section near the end of the *Iliad* where Hector, the Trojans' greatest warrior, has stepped out in front of the walls of Troy—before all the Trojans—to take on Achilles, the unstoppable, ruthless Greek hero; he is terrified, and he knows he will surely die. Eventually, he runs, and swift-footed Achilles catches him, kills him, and brutally mistreats his corpse.[7] One of Dr. Gregory's prompts for this paper was this:

> Consider the death of Hector in Book 22: his meditation before the gates of Troy in hearing of his parents, his behavior before Achilles and his flight, and his final confrontation with him. How does this final episode express Hector's specific role within Troy and his specific character? Does he die nobly?[iii]

Now, this prompt might seem daunting to you at first, as it would have been to me as an eighteen-year-old freshman from a pretty so-so suburban public high school. But let's take another look. The first sentence just tells us what passages Dr. Gregory wants us to focus on—the section of the text where Hector thinks about the confrontation with Achilles, how Hector then behaves, and the final battle and his death. But the next sentence is interesting. It asks a question: How does this episode express, first, Hector's role in Troy and, second, Hector's character? Then there's a second question: Does he die nobly?

What's being asked here? That question "How does an episode express *x*?" does not seem like one from the Four Arguments. But if we rephrase it in terms of stasis theory, it becomes more clear:

- What is Hector's role in Troy?
- What is Hector's character?
- How does the episode express those two things—that is, how does it cause us to understand those aspects of his character and role?
- Does he die a good death—a noble death?

iii Used with permission of Dr. Eileen Gregory.

When you look at it this way, you probably can see how stasis theory can help us. The first two are *definitional* questions, right? They are asking "What is Hector?" under two auspices: What is his role, and what is his character? The third is a subtly *causal* question, asking us to show how the images, diction, and other wordplay express those things to us, or cause us to understand. Then the fourth question is an *evaluative* one: Is his death good and noble? So we can see that Dr. Gregory is asking for a pretty complex paper. To answer her prompt, we must stack two definitional arguments, one after the other, then move on to a causal argument, and finally use all of that to lead to an evaluative argument. We might have to do something like this:

- Hector's role in Troy is to be the greatest military fighter, the only one to match against the greatest of the Greeks, Achilles.
- Hector's character is grand: courageous, fierce, loyal, and so on.
- We know this because the text says *x*, *y*, and *z*.

(Or we could reverse these, starting with describing Hector's actions, showing how these illustrate his character, and explaining how that character allows him to fill the role as the greatest of the Trojan heroes. Now that I look at it, I like this organization better . . .) Finally, you would lead to the destination of the entire argument, the evaluative one:

- Hector's death is noble because, in his death, he is *a*, *b*, *c*, and *d* (your criteria for a noble death), or
- Hector's death is pitiful and ignoble; despite his grand and noble life before this, he dies running from Achilles, frightened and lost.
    - Here is where you would again use the evidence from the episode, showing how that episode expresses his

> ultimate end, his final character, and your summative judgment about him.

So stasis theory is in fact useful for answering this prompt. We just had to figure out what Dr. Gregory was asking in terms of the Four Arguments and decide how to stack them one upon the other.

Let's try another one from Dr. Gregory—a second option for the same paper:

> The Achaians [what Homer calls the Greeks in the *Iliad*] have great men other than Achilles, who are distinguished by their own distinct excellences. Discuss one of these, indicating his distinct excellence by contrast with that of others, and the way in which it contributes to the good of the whole. Be specific in reference to episodes and passages from the book. In this regard consider, for instance, Nestor, Aias, or Odysseus.[iv]

Again, the first sentence just tells us what to look at—any Greek hero other than Achilles—and the last sentence even suggests three possibilities for us. The third sentence reminds us of something we should already know: that we need to ground our arguments in solid evidence. The second sentence is the one with the real prompt. We have to be careful, though: "Discuss"? What does that mean? It's too general to give much guidance. But later in the sentence we get some direction: We are to talk about one hero and what excellence makes him distinct, and we are invited to do this by contrasting him with others. Then we have to show how his excellence "contributes to the good of the whole." Are you with me? Are you a step ahead? What kinds of arguments do we have here? Let's take a look by picking out one hero and thinking through what questions we have. Let's say we take the first hero on the list, Nestor. Now, Nestor is the oldest

iv Used with permission of Dr. Eileen Gregory.

among the heroes who have gone to Greece, and while he therefore does not take part in much of the fighting, he offers a lot of advice to the younger leaders by drawing on his experience. So if we were to articulate an answer to the question, we might say something like this:

- Nestor is older, so he's not a great fighter like the other Greeks; his distinct excellence is his wisdom.
  - That's definitional, right? It's answering the question "What is Nestor?" or "What is Nestor like—what is his particular excellence?"; "Nestor is wise" is the simplest form of this argument's thesis.
- Nestor's wisdom contributes to the good of the Greeks by *a*, *b*, *c*, and *d*.
  - Hmm. "Contributes"—that's causal! We're being asked to argue how Nestor is a contributing cause to the overall good of the Greek army.

So by reading the prompt carefully—often this means reading the *verbs* of the prompt carefully—we can rephrase it into one of the four questions of stasis theory and see what we need to do. We need to start with a definitional argument and then lead to a causal argument.

Let's try another prompt, from my estimable colleague Andrew Osborn, this time about *Beowulf.* As you might know, one of the questions of that poem is whether its values are Christian or pagan. Dr. Osborn asks students to consider how the Christian poet regards the pagan content of the culture he is describing:

> Organize an argument . . . by considering to what extent the *Beowulf* poet's Christian sensibilities alienate him from his subject or whether he is able to reconcile the quest for martial glory with Christian motives and attributes.[v]

v Used with permission of Dr. Andrew Osborn.

This one gives us two possible theses by which to respond, right?

- The poet's Christian sensibilities alienate him from his pagan subject matter, or
- The poet is able to reconcile the quest for martial glory with his Christian attitudes.

Can you see what kind of argument this is? Look at the verbs: "alienate," "reconcile." Which of the four questions do they address? If you are alienated, something caused you to move from one state to another, from feeling like you are part of something to feeling apart from it. And if you reconcile two things, you create an effect where two things come together. So in the first sample thesis, we have to show how the poet's Christian sensibilities *cause* him to pull away from pagan values, and in the second, we have to show how the poet is able to *cause* his Christian sensibilities to come together with the pagan notions of martial glory. Bingo.

Finally, let's try a poem analysis. Dr. Osborn asked his students to write about the following questions on Shakespeare's Sonnet 29 ("When, in disgrace with fortune and men's eyes"):[vi]

---

vi Here's the full text of the sonnet:
When, in disgrace with fortune and men's eyes,
I all alone beweep my outcast state
And trouble deaf heaven with my bootless cries
And look upon myself and curse my fate,
Wishing me like to hone more rich in hope,
Featur'd like him, like him with friends possess'd,
Desiring this man's art and that man's scope,
With what I most enjoy contented least;
Yet in these thoughts myself almost despising,
Haply I think on thee, and then my state,
Like to the lark at break of day arising
From sullen earth, sings hymns at heaven's gate;
For thy sweet love remember'd such wealth brings
That then I scorn to change my state with kings.

1. What problem is the speaker considering here? What precisely is the state of mind he sees in himself? Be sure to base your thought here on the actual language of the poem.
2. The last portion of the poem introduces a "you" ("thee"). What relation to the speaker does this person seem to have, and what is his significance within this moment of the speaker's experience? Explain the importance of the simile in lines 11–12: What exactly is being compared to what?
3. This poem is a sonnet. What kind? How do the divisions in the sonnet form correspond with the movement of thought in the poem? How is the problem described in the first quatrain extended in the second? What is the shift in thought in the third quatrain (beginning on line 9)? Does the final couplet resolve the initial problem in any way?[vii]

By now you might be able to see that the first question is all about defining things: the speaker's problem is *x*; the speaker's state of mind is *y*. Then in the second question, we move from a definitional argument (the relationship between the speaker and "thee" is *z*; its significance is *a*, *b*, or *c*) to a kind of causal argument: What meaning does the simile create? Then, to answer the third question, we have to move from a definitional argument (this is an English sonnet; the quatrains fit the parts of the thought) to causal arguments (the poet shifts the thought at line nine; he uses the couplet to resolve the problem by doing *a*, *b*, and *c*). And you might notice that there is a kind of implicit evaluative argument here: If the poem's causes (its words and images) lead artfully to its effects (the meanings and ideas it is trying to convey), then it is a good poem.

vii Used with permission of Dr. Andrew Osborn.

Could we write the paper showing that the poem makes a problem/solution argument? That is an interesting idea. The sonnet really does break down this way: "When I'm alone and depressed [problem], I think about you [solution], and then I feel much better; I wouldn't change my place with kings." Perhaps describing how the *poem*'s argument works can illustrate how Shakespeare conveys his meaning.

It appears, then, that writing literary criticism—interpreting a text—does indeed use the Four Arguments of stasis theory, but it groups them in complex ways. I was comforted, and pleased, to see how stasis theory could help us understand what is going on as we build arguments about novels, poems, and plays. And as I read my colleagues' prompts, I thought, "What difficult things we ask of our freshmen!" To expect students to recognize different kinds of arguments and stack them one after another in the best order is a challenging task. Even when I teach each of the Four Arguments *by themselves*, it often takes students a few attempts to see how each of the different structures work; you know from working through this book how much work it takes to be able to combine them in these sophisticated ways. But students are able to write these kinds of arguments, with some coaching by wonderful professors such as Dr. Gregory and Dr. Osborn, and you can as well. This is a challenge, but perhaps that is why reading literature, including demanding texts such as the *Iliad* and *Beowulf*, and then writing about them leads to huge leaps in students' powers of analysis. This is one good reason to have literature as a requirement for every student: It asks you to engage with reality in incredibly complex ways, challenging your thinking about other people, their motivations, and their actions. If you can argue about literature in complex but clear ways, you can argue about anything. As you begin to master stasis theory, then, you should feel confident that you can take this discipline into any field and use the Four Arguments to speak and write effectively.

AFTERWORD

STASIS THEORY FOR THE REAL WORLD—AND FOR YOUR HUMANITY

If you have not merely read through this book but *worked* with it, trying the exercises, learning the four templates until they are almost second nature, and testing different arguments in these different patterns, I have the utmost confidence that you are significantly better at building arguments than when you started reading this book just a short time ago. Your ability to read and critically analyze others' arguments, I am sure, has improved as well. Take a quick look back at the introduction's "What Kind of Argument Am I?" quiz and see how much more quickly you grasp those arguments—and how easily you can map out a rough outline for each of them. This knowledge will help you in every class you take.

But do not think that you will leave behind stasis theory after you graduate; this theory, two thousand years ago in ancient Rome, was devised not for schoolwork but for training lawyers, political orators, and others out in the real world. Today you will find it essential to your career. Why? Well, we live in an information economy, correct? The stock market, the economy, almost every profession now is tied to a global tidal wave of information that, if we are not careful, can completely overwhelm us. What are the skills that lead to success in such an information economy? They include the following:

- Being able to sift through information quickly and find what is relevant and what is not
- Identifying the most important questions and issues in that content
- Judging what is valid and not, true and not, in the way people address those questions
- Understanding those issues in contexts and seeing how they affect later outcomes
- Creating your own analysis of these questions and issues
- Communicating your take on all of this to others

What I have shown you is how stasis theory takes you through that process. If you can see what kind of arguments people are making all around you, you will master the first two bullet points, and the next four will soon follow. As you home in on a particular argument—a business proposal, for instance—you will be able to evaluate it and determine whether it defines the problem clearly and whether it argues well for its proposed solution, covering the question of feasibility and showing how the proposal is better than other solutions. When you communicate your analysis with others, you will have the sound rhetorical structure to give you confidence in building and presenting your arguments.

When alumni visit my office, telling me of their lives and their careers, many of them share some version of the following story: They were in a business meeting with people from different departments and offices and were the only ones continually asking questions, making comments, uncovering problems in the proposals, and offering their own solutions. Later, they say, their boss's boss, or a director from another office, or someone from another firm asked their boss, "Who was that? She was the only person asking good questions!" and "Who was the one who wrote that report? Wow, that youngster can write really clearly." The next time that person has an opening, guess who is at the top of his list? The youngster who could quickly digest, analyze, and communicate. "That is how," a recent graduate told me, "I became the vice president of marketing in my company before I was twenty-seven years old." He went on to say, "In New York City, all of the people hired for marketing jobs are Ivy Leaguers, and yet here was I, getting promoted over them. All that stuff you guys say about the Core Curriculum, reading literature, and a liberal education? It is true."

And to pick up a point I made in the introduction, you don't want AI doing this for you. You want to make your own arguments and analyze those of others for yourself because you want to be able to deploy those arguments well in any situation, whether you have a powerful computer in your pocket (or hand) or not.

The Point of It All

But the point of learning the Four Arguments is not simply to be successful in your career, to get that promotion, to have a nice house and drive a shiny new car. Those things would be nice, to be sure. But they're not why we learn rhetoric, or why I have taught you stasis theory. We learn how to argue because, as Aristotle notes, as humans we seek out the truth; we want to know the truth, and when we grasp it, we want to lead others to that truth. That is the point of rhetoric: to argue our way past mere opinion to the truth of reality. To return to an example from earlier in this book, no one argues for more parking spaces just to win an argument; you present this argument to the administration because it is *true* that the parking situation has become a real problem and you think you have grasped the *truth* of a solution that will make it better for you and everyone else. Or to take a more nuanced example: When football coaches argue that (predominantly female) cheerleaders are athletes, that argument in itself might be a good one, but if we see that they are arguing this in order to protect their own (predominantly male) teams under Title IX, not because it is the truth, we recognize that they are not pursuing truth but self-interest instead, and so we no longer trust their motives or their desire for truth.

As we seek the truth, and grasp it, and cling to it, we grow as people, because this is our final cause: to seek truth and form our lives around it. Arguing well is, to my mind and Aristotle's, one of the best ways to begin that process. Achieving what Aristotle calls *eudaimonia*— "full human flourishing"—starts with discovering, speaking, and living in the truth. (Again, this is why you don't want AI doing this for you.) I hope this slim book has helped you on the path to your own human flourishing.

APPENDIX ONE

THE TEMPLATES FOR THE FOUR ARGUMENTS

Definitional Arguments

I. Define the predicate
II. Show that the subject fits in the category of the predicate

Causal Arguments

I. Describe fully the phenomenon or event whose cause you are examining
II. Then either
   a. Lead us to understand the chain of events that led to this, or
   b. Lead us to understand the effects that came out of this
III. While also
   a. Eliminating false causes, those factors that people may think were part of the chain of causality, but in actuality were not

Five Different Templates for Causal Arguments

TEMPLATE 2.1
Effect Stems from Causes A, B, C, and D

I. Describe the situation, phenomenon, or event
II. Explore causes
   a. Depending on the types of causes, you might want to group them:
      i. Which causes were remote and which were proximate?
      ii. Which were the necessary causes?
      iii. Which were sufficient?
      iv. Which were contributing factors?
      v. Was there any precipitating cause?
III. Eliminate false causes

TEMPLATE 2.2
Cause A Leads to Effect B, Which Becomes Cause B, Which leads to Effect C, Which Becomes Cause C, Which Leads to Effect D…

I. Describe the phenomenon
   a. Start at the end of the chain: the ultimate result, e.g., the student's horrible grades leading to his dropping out of college
II. Go back to the moment before the most remote cause—before any of the effects had happened
   a. E.g., describe a time when the student was happy and doing well in classes
III. Start with the most remote cause
   a. E.g., the student moved to a new dorm and fell in with a new group of friends who were bad influences
IV. Work forward down the chain of causes and effects, leading back to the phenomenon

TEMPLATE 2.3
Cause Leads to Effects A, B, and C

I. Describe the cause
  a. Give a picture of what happened (or is happening)
  b. Ask: What happened as a result?

II. Describe effect A
  a. Was the cause a contributing, necessary, sufficient, or precipitating cause of this effect?
  b. How can you be sure the cause was a cause of this effect?

III. Describe effect B
  a. Was the cause a contributing, necessary, sufficient, or precipitating cause of this effect?
  b. How can you be sure the cause was a cause of this effect?

IV. Describe effect C
  a. Was the cause a contributing, necessary, sufficient, or precipitating cause of this effect?
  b. How can you be sure the cause was a cause of this effect?

V. And so on, until you have described all the effects you wish to describe (You might want to describe only one effect; that's okay.)

VI. Eliminate false causes/effects, especially if there are popularly held ideas that your research has shown to be wrong

TEMPLATE 2.4
The Single Difference

I. Describe all of the commonalities in your two (or three, or however many) subjects
    a. E.g., two brothers: all the things that are alike in them, their upbringing, etc.
II. Describe the very different results (or effects)
III. Identify the single difference that led to the different effects, despite all the other commonalities
    a. Show why this single effect caused the difference

TEMPLATE 2.5
The Common Factor

I. Identify the different instances of a single phenomenon
    a. E.g., American Legion men all dying of similar symptoms
    b. Show how different they all seem to be (e.g., geographically) and yet how alike they are in some crucial way
        i. E.g., very different people all with the same disease
II. Identify the common factor that unites all these instances
    a. Argue for this commonality and thus its cause of the phenomenon

Evaluative Arguments

I. Describe the subject
    a. Give a sense of the subject (without giving everything away)
    b. Establish your authority by using the terms and concepts of this field
    c. Establish yourself as a fair and objective judge
II. Offer a judgment (that is, your thesis)
    a. Answer the question, is it good or bad?
    b. Qualify your judgment as necessary

III. Show that the subject fits the criteria
    a. Criterion 1
        i. How it fits this criterion
    b. Criterion 2
        i. How it fits this criterion
    c. Criterion 3
        i. How it fits this criterion
    d. Criterion 4
        i. How it fits this criterion

And so forth, until you have explored all of your criteria.

IV. Answer any remaining counterarguments against your judgment

Problem/Solution Arguments

I. Describe the problem
    a. If it is well known, be brief and just remind the reader
    b. If it is not well known, set up the problem:
        i. Define the problem, and/or
        ii. Describe what caused it and its negative effects, and/or
        iii. Show that it is not good by showing how it does not measure up to criteria for this situation/process/activity
II. Articulate your solution
    a. Make it as specific and concrete as possible
    b. Show how it will solve the problem
        i. How it will remove the causes, or lead to good effects
        ii. How it will meet the criteria

c. Show that the solution is feasible
    i. Do you have the financial resources?
    ii. Do you have the human resources in time and talent?
d. What incentives does the audience have for implementing this solution?
e. Show that it is better than other solutions
f. Deal with any remaining questions/counterarguments
    i. Consider other practical questions
    ii. Consider philosophical questions, especially aesthetic and ethical ones

APPENDIX TWO

FINDING A THESIS AND THE FOUR TESTS OF A GOOD THESIS

I. **How do you get a good thesis in the first place?**

You might have come up with a general idea for a paper—"I'd like to do something about ^"—and yet you might struggle to make it to the next stage: finding a focus for your thoughts and an angle into the problems, issues, and questions surrounding that topic. Here are two ways to develop your thoughts.

a. [Good] Scratch an itch.

Some of the best advice I've ever received about getting ideas for a paper came from a graduate school professor of mine, the late Hoyt Duggan. He used to put on his best Texan accent from his youth and say, "You got to scratch where it itches."[i] What he meant was this: Just start with what is bugging you about a topic. I tell my students to ask, "What's making me itchy about this?" (What makes you itch might be different than what makes someone else itch—good!) Then scratch

i Astute readers might catch a reference to Cacciaguida in Dante's *Divine Comedy*.

that itch, and keep at it until you start to see an idea emerge.

When I was a student, I didn't do this. Instead, I would often start, largely unconsciously, with trying to figure out what my teacher wanted me to get out of the subject. That's not independent thinking; it's trying to out-guess someone else and then please them. Now, it takes confidence to say "I don't really get this" in the face of an important book or well-known scholar. But that's how good thinking gets started. One of the first itches I ever scratched was when I went to Europe and saw that none of the schools had sports teams. As a student-athlete, I noticed this and started itching, looking around for reasons why.

b. [Better] Ask a good question.

Saying "I don't get this" or "This makes me itchy" is a start, but it might not get you to a thesis. Good theses come from good questions. When you ask a good question, you are getting involved in the issues and controversies about that subject—and when you answer your question, you force yourself to take a side, a position. By asking and answering a question, you make a claim, and now you must defend that claim. That is what a thesis is: a claim, a position, your proposed answer to a question. But it needs to be a good question. Don't ask simple yes or no, either/or questions; these tend to produce flat, uninteresting answers and thus boring theses. I find that asking "What?," "How?," and "Why?" about your issue leads to very interesting answers. Practice this verbally at first with a friend, exploring these three questions about your topic.

To return to my example above, I started to ask, how did sports get mixed up with education in America? Why are sports teams such an integral part of the education landscape in America? Why don't Europeans do it this way? How does this affect how we fund, support, and think of education differently than Europeans do?

c. [Better] Use stasis theory.
   By using stasis theory, you can move from a general idea about a topic to a clear view of where the issues and disagreements are and where you can enter into the controversy. Stasis theory gives you a particular set of questions to ask in a particular order, helping you to ask more specific questions and find the nub of the issue. So run through the four questions of stasis theory and see how they help you focus your concerns. Ask, "What is this thing?" or "To what category does this thing belong?" or "What is like this thing?" Are there any issues, controversies, or problems over the definition of your subject? You might find, as with the question of whether cheerleaders are athletes, that there are a number of issues here. Or you might find no issues, and you can safely move on. Then ask, "What caused this or what effects did it have?" You might find that the issues surrounding this topic are about causes and effects—how it came about, or what it changed later on. Next ask, "Is it good or bad, worthwhile or not worth our time, pretty good or excellent?" These questions might lead you to see that here is where people struggle and argue about this topic. Finally, ask, "What should be done about this?" You might find that

the real issue is one of policy—what needs to be done about a problem.

I started to realize that what I wanted to explore was a causal question—a historical question: When and how did American schooling and American sports get mixed up with one another? And what were, and have been, the effects of this combination? Then came an evaluative question: Has this been a good thing or a bad thing for American education? Now I had a number of potential topics to explore and theses to articulate.

II. **Once you have a thesis, how do you know you have a good one?**

   Over the years, students have told me they have found my four tests of a good thesis to be very helpful.[ii] These tests should be used in the order presented below.

   a. Can a reasonable person disagree with it?
      i. If no one can disagree with your statement, then either you are merely stating facts or you are stating something so obvious or noncontroversial, that there's nothing to persuade anyone about. "Hitler was a bad guy" is not a thesis. Nor is "Jane Austen uses characterization, diction, and imagery in *Pride and Prejudice*."

ii A fellow graduate student taught me the first two questions many years ago, when we were both graduate teaching assistants in the University of Virginia's English department. I remember his dissertation, which was on composition and rhetoric, was to be titled "Common Sense." That notion—that almost everything we teach about writing is just helping students use their common sense—has stuck with me, as have these first two tests of a good thesis. I added tests three and four through my own experience.

b. Does it stand a chance of gaining the reader's agreement by the end of the paper?
   Notice there are actually two tests here: the reasonableness test and the focus test.
   i. Reasonableness: You can have a test that passes the first test but is so outrageous that no one is ever going to agree with it. "Hitler was a sweet guy" definitely passes the first test but does not pass the second.
   ii. Focus: Some theses pass both of these tests, but they would require covering so much material that they are a great thesis for a full book, not a four-page paper. Be sure that you can persuade the reader of your argument within the space of your assignment.

c. Does it have subordination?
   There should be one or more subordinate clauses in your thesis: "Although Dickens appears to *x*, he really *y*." "Before Grant decided *a* and *b*, he was forced to consider *c*, and this is why it is obvious that *d* was his real goal." Subordinate clauses build complex relationships into your claims—relationships of time, cause, and evaluation. They also show the parts of your argument.

d. You can see an implicit outline in the thesis statement. Since your thesis statement has subordination, you should be able to see the different parts of your argument and their relationship to one another. If the structure is "although *x*, really *y*," you know that you will have to establish the apparent reality of *x*, but then show that this is not the truth, or at least the full truth; the full truth is *y*. So if you have a good thesis that passes the first three tests, it should be fairly simple to build an outline that orders the points and subpoints of your paper.

NOTES FOR TEACHERS

CHAPTER ONE

1 The idea that definitions are just "the facts" and are already settled—you can just look them up in the dictionary—is deeply engrained in some students, so I encourage you to spend some time in class disabusing your students of this notion. The best way to do so is to give them examples, as I have done here, and get the class arguing for different viewpoints. They will quickly see that definitions are not settled matters and that persuading others of definitions can have important consequences. For instance, students realize that very different evidence will be brought before the court if this parking-lot-fight case becomes a self-defense case as opposed to a simple assault case. Perhaps you can use an issue in your own classroom or community to get this discussion started. Or you can discuss the controversial issue of how to charge police officers who cause the deaths of citizens—since charging requires that we define the acts of these police officers. Grand juries have responded to individual cases in very different ways, sometimes charging with major crimes, sometimes with lesser crimes, and sometimes with no charges at all.

2 Full disclosure: Fahnestock and Secor include a student essay on a similar topic: Jill Henkel, "Cheerleading: A Sport or an Activity?" Henkel argues that the cheerleaders' photos should appear in the sports section of the school yearbook, not the activities section. See Jeanne Fahnestock and Marie Secor, *A Rhetoric of Argument*, 3rd ed., (McGraw-Hill, 2004), 165–67. Ramage, Bean, and Johnson also mention the issue of whether cheerleaders are athletes. See John D. Ramage and John C. Bean, *Writing Arguments: A Rhetoric with Readings*, 4th ed. (Longman, 2006), 204. Funny—we teachers of argument all seem to have this question on our minds. I cannot trace back to my original thinking—was I already influenced by these books and then found the *Atlanta Journal-Constitution* article, or was I independently struck by the controversy and then found the arguments in these textbooks?

3 I find that many students are only vaguely aware of Title IX and its regulations, so you might have to explain the basics here—that it is a federal mandate originally intended to bring parity in educational programs for men and women, including but not limited to athletic programs. In some places, less-popular men's sports have been cut and women's sports added to achieve the balance the federal statute requires. The

Obama administration used Title IX in the field of sexual assault and harassment on college campuses.

4 I include these subjects here not to demand that teachers discuss them in class—it's your class and you know best what you would like to accomplish there—but only to show that some of the most controversial subjects of our time are rooted in definitional arguments. If you do discuss these topics, I encourage you to focus not on the particular positions but instead on how those discussing the issue define the important terms and what the implications are of those definitions.

5 For those who want to learn more about definitions, Sister Miriam Joseph's *The Trivium*, chapter 4, is a wonderful guide (Paul Dry Books, 2002), 71–89. She offers many more types of definition: distinctive definitions, causal definitions, descriptive definitions, definitions by example, and grammatical and rhetorical or nominal definitions, the last of which include definitions by etymology, definitions by synonyms, and arbitrary definitions. Fahnestock and Secor talk about definition by synonym, the genus/difference definition (what I am calling the stipulative definition), definition by example, the etymological definition, the genetic or historical definition, the negative definition, the figurative definition, the ostensive definition, and the operational definition. All of these are important to know if you want to become an expert at these arguments. For now, I want to keep it simple for students.

6 I cannot emphasize enough the importance of using this language of "the tasks to be successful": I urge you to use it over and over with your students. Far too often students think writing is a matter of figuring out "what each teacher wants" and giving the teacher that imaginary thing. This attitude turns writing into a kind of spy game: The student is a secret agent trying to ferret out the teacher's unspoken thoughts and desires. Changing the language to "the tasks that you need to accomplish to be successful at persuading someone" does away with the notion of "what the teacher wants" and the notion that every teacher wants something different. I find that students relax; they are grateful to learn that writing is not some elaborate mind game.

7 And of course that is the point—if I put only noncontroversial definitional claims here, it would lead the students right back into thinking that definitions are not really subjects for argumentation. It is a great practice to run through a few of these topics in class, asking students how they would organize the paper based on the argument. Some students see it very quickly—define the predicate; show that the subject fits in the category of the predicate—but others take more time. Since a few of these are "double-definition arguments," it can be fun to work from the simpler ones to the more complex ones. I encourage you to have students brainstorm their own arguments, but if they are having trouble doing so, they can discuss some of the ones I have reproduced here from students' work in my classes.

8 This argument actually took place during the Reagan administration; the issue was student lunches (especially free student lunches) and what to count as a vegetable in those lunches. It was reported with a great amount of derision in the mainstream media. Yet it emerged again in the Obama administration.

9 A controversial topic, to be sure, with implications for the treatment of alcoholism. This is one of the "double-definition" topics, as both "condition" and "disease" will have to be defined as predicates, and then the writer must show that alcoholism fits into one category and not the other.

10 This one is based on certain statements Lincoln made early in his political career up through the Lincoln–Douglas debates. Students who want to work on this one will want to dive into what Lincoln said about race.

11 Time for a silly one! Often students begin to see the structure of definitional arguments when they are not emotionally invested in the subject matter (as they might be about Abraham Lincoln as a racist, for instance). I once had a student work diligently on the question of whether an Oreo is a cookie or a biscuit, and she learned a great deal about the form of these arguments.

12 This is an interesting one, not just for subject matter that is so controversial today, or for the student's attempt to tease out different ways of getting at these issues, but also because there are three subjects (sex, gender, and social gender traits) and really no predicate ("things"?). Can this argument work? Students might want to tease out different ways of stating this thesis to help them be more effective. They might conceive of sex, gender, and social gender traits as the predicate, but then what is the subject? Maybe "aspects of the human person"?

13 Another silly one, but it can produce good work. I never asked my student why he was arguing this particular topic, but I can imagine the context that produced this thesis: A teenager is told by a parent, "You can't wear those flip-flops tonight—*flip-flops are not shoes!*" Can the teenager best the parent in this discussion? It depends on his skill in organizing and executing the argument.

14 This issue burst onto the scene at the University of Dallas a few years ago as part of a larger discussion of modesty in women's dress. A similar debate erupted at the University of Notre Dame in 2019, when a woman on a college visit with her daughter wrote a letter to the editor of the campus newspaper complaining that many of the female students wore leggings as pants to Catholic Mass. The writer criticized these women for what she thought was their sexually suggestive or revealing dress in front of young men. The letter led to an organized day wherein many female students at Notre Dame deliberately wore leggings as a sort of protest. I find this amusing because during the fourteenth century in England—the period of my professional expertise—preachers thundered about young *men* wearing their gowns so short that their legging-covered buttocks could be seen, saying that this enticed *women* (who in the day were

the ones seen as unable to control their sexual impulses) to sin. When describing the young, flighty, flirtatious Squire in the General Prologue to *The Canterbury Tales*, Chaucer includes the detail "short was his gowne" to suggest that the Squire is a "lovyere and a lusty bacheler." *Plus ça change…*

15 The student who made this argument was responding to one of my provocative pedagogical irritations when I teach definitional arguments. To get my students interested in definitions, and invested in defending their own, I often tell them Roper's Definition of a Sport. The first thing, I say, is that it has to have an objective method of scoring. Either the ball goes over the line or it doesn't; either you cross the line before me or you don't. Now, referees are human and can make mistakes, but in the theory of the sport there must be an objective way of scoring: The puck goes between the two posts, below the crossbar, and over the line. I tell them that this part of the definition comes from my irritated response to figure skating, where I used to hear commentators all the time say things like "That was wonderful, but they can't give her too high a score, because they have to leave room for *x*," the supposedly truly excellent skater who was coming later. So sorry, divers and gymnasts and even ski jumpers, all of whose sports rely on subjective judging: You are amazing athletes, but you are not playing a sport. All of those X Games events, like trick snowboarding? Not sports.

This riles up the students to offer a counterdefinition, and I have achieved my goal, but I do not stop there. My next requirement is that "You have to get your heartbeat over 120 beats a minute regularly while playing it, or it's not a sport." Sometimes I'll suggest a restatement of this to college students: "It's not a sport if you can drink beer while doing it." So chess is a wonderful game, but it's not a sport, and neither are darts or (here's where I really annoy some) golf. I'll freely admit, I say, that golf is a wonderful *game* and that golfers have a great deal of skill and talent and ability (none of which I will ever possess). But as a former soccer player I have to hold the line on this one. A sport should involve constant strenuous physical activity. You can't play soccer or rugby or full-court basketball or any other actual sport, I'll prod them, while drinking beer—you'll very soon vomit. *Q.E.D.*

Then I sit back and let the students argue it out. If no one will take up my cause, I will continue my devil's advocate pose and let them see how carefully they need to define their terms if they are going to use terms like *sport* as the predicate.

16 I have never seen this film, so I wasn't aware of this as a joke cultural issue, but students find this one amusing. In fact, with no prompting of my own, this topic has come up multiple times when students brainstorm for a definitional topic.

17 Okay, I have to admit, a doctoral student created this one. I include it to show how even at the highest academic level (maybe *especially* at the

highest academic level), interesting definitional arguments are happening all the time.

18 Unlike other argumentation textbooks, this book will provide one classic argument at the end of each chapter. These are more for an extra challenge—for fun and profit—than anything else. I include them so your students can see how stasis theory might help them read classic texts with new eyes—as arguments the characters or speakers are making, with the authors inviting them to explore and critique the characters' arguments. And of course I hope these selections will draw students into exploring the text as a whole and show them how much fun it is to think through literary texts.

CHAPTER TWO

1 As you work through the arguments, it is important to show students how stasis theory sequences the arguments. You should not have much difficulty getting a discussion going about causal arguments once students understand the term. You can have a quick brainstorming session where you list all kinds of causal arguments on the board by giving the students general topics: "sports...go!," "situations here at school...go!," "things at your house...go!," and so forth. Students quite naturally are interested in causes and, with prompting, in effects, too. Ask them, "What happened as a result of...?" and they will get moving quickly. To vary the dynamic, have them brainstorm in small groups and write their topics on the board at the end of a short period (about five minutes). If they are stuck, you can always have them skip ahead in the chapter to Exercise 3.1, where I list some of my own students' causal theses. Often just seeing others' topics gets the creative juices flowing.

2 Here again you can use students' own interests and expertise to help them generate topics. Hobbies, family businesses and cultural backgrounds, sports, political issues—all are grist for the mill. The better you know your students, the better you can encourage them to invent causal arguments about the subjects they know and love.

3 If you wish, you could even make one of these topics the central topic you and the class explore together as you work through this chapter. It could be pedagogically useful to have the entire class working on one topic together—researching, ferreting out false causes and dead-end narratives, adding pieces to the puzzle. Or you could model such an investigation by working on one such topic while allowing students to work on their own interests.

4 So much of the fun of leading discussions in this chapter is continually pointing out what causal factors or effects the students have not yet considered. All you need do is say, "Oh? And what caused that? Were those the only factors involved?" Or "Really?—that was the only consequence of that decision? Didn't it also affect this other group?" Doing this in an encouraging way is the trick—so students are motivated to keep investigating the

causes and effects more completely and not overwhelmed by the complexity of what they are attempting to understand.

5 Full disclosure: Lunsford, Ruszkiewicz, and Walters, in *Everything's an Argument*, seventh edition, have a nice chart on page 251 showing the differences between these kinds of causes and providing examples. (At one point they use "loss of oxygen" as a sufficient cause for death, rather than my "loss of a sufficient amount of blood." And they use "fuel is necessary for fire" but do not mention heat and oxygen.) But this is a standard list of the types of causes that anyone discussing this subject knows.

6 This is a great place to take the topics students have already brainstormed and ask them to explore proximate and remote causes of their chosen events. And if you have a common topic you are investigating together—as I will do here with World War II—you can have the entire class explore proximate and remote causes. Write the students' responses on the board in two columns, "proximate" and "remote." As you walk through the different kinds of causes, be sure to keep using both their topics and yours as examples.

7 I encourage you to spend considerable time with the distinction between necessary, sufficient, precipitating, and contributing causes. In my experience, some students struggle to catch on to these distinctions until they have reviewed a number of examples. But once they do understand, these four concepts help them in their thinking, both in academic topics and in their daily lives.

8 When students begin to organize their causal arguments, they see how much more complicated these arguments are than definitional arguments. Here I give one fundamental set of tasks that a causal argument must accomplish, but next I will give not one template or pattern, as I did for definitional arguments, but three...and in a few pages, two more, for a total of five templates! Students, however, seem to adjust to this greater complexity once they see that different kinds of problems call forth different organizational patterns. Still, as students come up with a topic and a thesis, make sure they see which template fits with their particular causal argument. I highly recommend that you require the students to submit a thesis to you so you can help identify which of the templates fits with what they want to accomplish.

9 Full disclosure: I learned these three patterns from Lunsford, Ruszkiewicz, and Walters, who work through them on pages 242–245 of *Everything's an Argument*, seventh edition. I explain them somewhat differently, however.

10 I like waiting to introduce research until this point, when students will need it, and I like how causal arguments encourage us to look beyond *mere book learnin'* for our knowledge and evidence. For nowhere is it as likely to challenge students to join traditional library research, modern online research, and old-fashioned gumshoe reporting as a good causal argument. For this reason, you might wish to have the causal argument be a long-term assignment, due later in the term, so you can allow the students time to explore their subject material. But I find that having

them submit something to me fairly early on—a tentative thesis and a possible outline based on the templates—allows me to ask them a host of questions that they have not considered, and to encourage them to do at least a bit of research to answer these questions. "You might want to talk to someone in the City Manager's Office about that," I might write. Or "You know that Dr. Sullivan has written articles on the Scottish Enlightenment and its effects on the Industrial Revolution, right? He might be able to help you tease out some of the causes here and suggest some you have overlooked." Or "How much time have you spent among the immigrant community? I know a senior English major who had an internship last summer working with a law firm that assists immigrants with their process of applying for legal status—do you want me to put her in touch with you?" Following up on any of these things takes time, so I put off the due date for the final causal paper until later in the term.

I don't want to turn this into an entire section on research methods and skills, but I will say that one of the most important shifts for a student to make is understanding that all the books and articles on a subject are *arguments*, just like the ones they are making, not necessarily "the definitive truth" on the subject. I tell them a bit about academic work, how we geeky academics go to conferences and deliver papers that are arguing with the other people in our field, and out of that publish articles and sometimes books—each of them still carrying on an argument. Sometimes I pass out my favorite cartoon from Vivian Scott Hixson's funny book of academic cartoons, *He Looks Too Happy to Be an Assistant Professor*. It shows a tweedy gentleman standing in front of a stack of books, and the bubble above his head says, "None of these idiots knows a *thing* about the problem!" Below is the comment "The start of another great book." If students can understand that—that the 350-page book about Milton's *Paradise Lost* is an argument with other Milton scholars, that the economics book on monetary policy is an argument between the Keynesians and the Austrians—then they will begin to approach their research with more energy, focus, and critical analysis. Even when they interview someone, they should have their antennae up, probing the subject for bias and subjective attitudes. I once crafted an assignment to get students to understand the argumentative nature of the materials in the library. The next day, a student—I can still see her; her name was Colleen—came into my office, and I could tell she was angry. "What's up?" I asked. "You know all those books in the library?" she started, her annoyance steaming out of her. "They don't tell the truth!" She had discovered, she said, that they were all just arguing with one another. "Sit down and let's talk about it," I said, pulling out a chair and saying, "You just grew up a bit today." (Now, does that mean none of the books had truth in them? No, and we discussed this. But she *had* made a big step forward in her intellectual development.)

11 Fahnestock and Secor credit John Stuart Mill for the concept of the single difference and the common factor, and they explore two others from Mill:

the method of varying causes and effects (when two things seem to vary together) and the elimination method (taking away all possible causes, leaving only one, which you then show is the cause). I prefer to keep to just the single difference and the common factor to show students how the concepts work, but if you like, you can explore these additional two. See *A Rhetoric of Argument*, third edition, 196–205.

12 You might encourage the students to brainstorm other single-difference situations. Help them to look for situations in which all the factors seem to be the same but the results are vastly different. Family dynamics are good here (perhaps birth order is the single difference?). So are student results—a class full of students who receive the same instruction but get different grades at the end of the semester. Or perhaps start with the effect: students admitted to very different colleges who came out of the same honors program at the same high school. Is it possible to find the single (significant) difference?

13 Again, you might gather the class and brainstorm potential topics for a common-factor causal argument. The trick is to find a group of people, the more disparate the better, experiencing the same thing, and begin to consider the common factor that might be causing the similar effects. Diseases, psychological conditions like anxiety, even teen suicide—all have been subject to attempts to find a common factor. But the brainstorming need not be all about negative effects. Books such as *Talent Is Overrated* by Geoff Colvin, *Mindset* by Carol Dweck, *Grit* by Angela Duckworth, and *Make It Stick* by Peter C. Brown, Henry L. Roediger III, and Mark A. McDaniel all take research from cognitive psychology, emotional intelligence, and more to explore the common factors among happy and successful people.

14 As in chapter 1, I recommend getting students to think quickly and openly when brainstorming—it is important for them to generate many topics and not engage in judging or critiquing them at this point. You might wish to have the class do the brainstorming together, or you might break the students into groups of three or four if that makes them feel more comfortable. At any rate, find some way to gather all of their ideas, writing them on the board or typing them up for the next class. Praise any and all of them at this stage, as much as you can, finding ways that they can see the potential papers that could come from them. "That would be a great series of articles in the local newspaper," I might say, or "Wow, you have a whole doctoral dissertation there," or "That's a really relevant issue today, isn't it? I'd love to see what you turn up as the causes." Later, you might work with the student to turn that dissertation-sized idea into a four-page paper, but at this stage, just coming up with ideas (of whatever size) is the point.

15 At this stage you will surely need to intervene. Here you will see in stark form whether the students understand the series of rhetorical tasks in front of them, whether they have ordered their argument well according to the templates, and whether they understand the evidence and reason-

ing they will need to deploy for each section of the template. These skills and abilities do not come automatically to most students, and many students need help seeing other factors and types of causes they have not considered. It might take several iterations of this process, moving from one of the five templates to an outline for the student's paper, before the organization is sound. But time invested here—by both the student and you, the instructor—pays many dividends later. When students get a clear template-outline, with a clear set of tasks to accomplish and the right kind of evidence deployed, they talk about the "actual writing" as so much easier, so much more manageable, than before. (I put "actual writing" in scare quotes because, of course, all of the stages are "writing," but students often do not see the acts of invention and organization as writing. The sooner they can see the entire process as "writing," the more progress they will make.)

16 In writing a paper, students often put pressure on themselves to deliver the definitive answer on a subject. But good, thoughtful, responsible writers—famous writers—often say, "I don't have all the answers here, but I do know this much." Letting them know this—and even pointing them to a few examples, if you like—can be an enormous relief to them and end up making them much more thoughtful participants in the conversation about whatever subject is important to them.

17 I offer these wider reflections as a way for students to think more broadly, more philosophically, about the concept of cause (and effect). You might present this material as time for open-ended fun discussions at the end of their hard work in this chapter. If you want to skip them, that is fine with me, but I hope not.

I find that students at first struggle with Aristotle's concept of the four causes, but as they come to understand them through examples, they realize how useful the distinctions are. You might take simple objects in the classroom—a desk, a file cabinet—and get students to run through the four causes in order to cement the concepts in their minds. Then reach out to larger, more abstract things—an automobile, a school, a city—and see whether they can explore the four causes of those things as well. I find that understanding what happened in the Early Modern period leading to the fact/value distinction can have powerful effects, curing them of a weak and unexamined relativism that prevents good thinking on important matters. Soon they are noting their classmates saying, "Well, that's just your opinion" and calling them out on it: "You're making the fact/value distinction there; why isn't my point valid?"

18 Again, the point of including these classic arguments at the end of the chapter is to provide an extra challenge and help students see how stasis theory can provide them with real insights into texts they might have thought opaque before. You might screen a scene or two leading up to Brutus's speech if you like, or just summarize what is happening and then let the students get to work on the speech. Often, Brutus's and Antony's speeches are contrasted in terms of the first using ethos (Brutus essentially

says, "You know me; you can trust me; I knew what I was doing, and I did it for your own good") while Antony trumps him with a masterful use of pathos. But note that Brutus's speech also functions as a causal defense of his actions: what steps led him to act. You might work the students through the speech: What were the contributing causes, according to Brutus? In recounting the steps that led to his action, what does Brutus leave out (which the audience saw in Acts 1–3)? What evidence does he give to support his argument? As we see in the ethos/pathos analysis, Brutus's reasoning is thin. His only argument seems to be "Caesar was ambitious, and this led me to kill him." Is ambition a *sufficient cause* for being murdered?

CHAPTER THREE

1 It is important to continue showing how stasis theory sequences the arguments. When students see that such discussions are not random, isolated topics, they understand how the arguments fit together and must be considered in a particular order to produce some progress.

If you have tired of my bar-fight example, please, by all means, choose another one. Classical literature is replete with great controversies where we ask evaluative questions: Did Achilles act in a good way? Did Hector die nobly? Or if you prefer more contemporary subjects, you might return to the climate-change debate I referenced earlier: once one has moved through the causes of climate change, the debate somewhat naturally moves to the question "How bad is it?" Here the two sides have long disagreed, with one side saying that we face a worldwide ecological disaster if we do not act very soon, or even immediately—or say we are already too late—and the other side arguing that none of this is as bad, or will be as bad, as the "doomsayers" predict.

2 I am not advocating violence here, only suggesting that, depending on the circumstances, opinions among the witnesses might be divided on whether the punch was a good thing or not. (I do not generally advocate violence as a way to solve problems, but neither do I rule it out in all circumstances. See Aristotle on courage as the mean between cowardice and foolhardiness.)

3 If you like, this could be a good place to explore Aristotle's distinction between *doxa* and *endoxa*. The former means "beliefs" or "opinions," and the latter suggests those ideas about which there is more or less a consensus because they have been tested by argument and debate. Aristotle does not say that the *endoxa* are necessarily true, but he does say that they must be considered more seriously than mere *doxa*. Think of a consensus about the best restaurants in town and a list of multiple-Oscar-winning films as being examples of *endoxa*.

4 This section is an important one to discuss in class—if for no other reason than to head off those students who want to hijack a thoughtful discussion with "that's just your opinion." By putting it in these terms, and multiplying examples of the ways in which they really do value the opinions of those with expertise, I have found that I can move students beyond the

unthinking relativism that infects so much of their mind-space and short-circuits so much good work they could do. But it takes strong examples, even extreme examples, at first: "You don't hire a plumber," I ask, "and then, when he tells you what is needed to fix the leak, say, 'That's just your opinion,' do you? Do you really think your opinion is equal to that of the plumber? If so, why are you paying him $150 an hour?" Beginning on this level of technical skill can lead students in the right direction. Gradually you can move to community questions, political questions, and aesthetic questions. Usually they balk at aesthetics, because they have imbibed the notion that any form of art—painting, sculpture, music, literature—is utterly subjective. But if you can get them to see that an experienced cellist knows things on which he can base his superior judgment of another cellist, the students slowly begin to crack open this closed-minded relativism. (It might be good to bring a cellist to the classroom on this day!) And if you can do that, perhaps—just perhaps—you can someday get beyond their relativism on moral questions, which is the Holy Grail of all this effort.

5 An easy way to show this to the students is to bring in two or three film or restaurant reviews and read only the first paragraph. Once you call their attention to this technique, students pick up on the ways a writer is establishing her authority and showing her objectivity. You can also have them practice in groups of three, talking through a subject they know well and having the auditors note the ways they are establishing authority and demonstrating their objectivity—or failing to do so.

6 Sorry for the reference to Harry Chapin's "Mr. Tanner," which is now surely quite obscure, but I couldn't resist. If you caught this, I crown you a very nerdy (and probably at least middle-aged) person.

7 If your students did not notice the implicit criteria, you might go back and have them ferret out the implied criteria for singing Schubert and for making a film about American men.

8 I used to think the process of finding criteria was easy, but over the years I have found that students often struggle with understanding criteria. So I encourage you to help students work through this next section. I found that students wanted to say good things about a particular restaurant but did not seem to understand that standards and criteria mean moving beyond particularities to more general levels of abstraction.

9 This is one of those moments when you can appeal to students' common practice. They understand that intention and audience and purpose shape the argument they are making, and they have had these arguments among themselves. "I'm not trying to say it's one of the best songs of all time," they probably have said, "but dang, it is one good funk groove." Or "Mr. Jones was not so great at teaching algebra, but man, he made physics so interesting—he's the best science teacher in the school." Each deploys different subgroupings, different purposes, different intentions, different theses, and different arguments.

10 Again I find it helps students to use that old creative writing chestnut "Write what you know," at least until they begin to master the *dispositio* and the needs of an evaluative argument.

11 Notice the lack of qualification in this first thesis. I wanted to start with a stark, universal statement; you might see how students respond to this. If they do not know volleyball, allow them to substitute in some athlete they do know who might be considered the GOAT—the Greatest of All Time—and see how much opposition they receive from classmates until they qualify it.

12 This is an interesting thesis to explore; the challenge here is surely to discover the criteria. What is the purpose of a system of government? By what criteria do we measure whether a system of government is good or bad? The intellectual work at this level is a wonderful challenge for students.

13 Hah. This student isn't pulling any punches in her hatred of Disney, is she? This thesis is a good one to show how a causal argument supports and leads to the evaluative argument that envelops it. Here the student will have to show the Disney movies as a cause, and lead us to see the bad psychological effects that come out of them, as the prime evidence that they are bad films. Implicit is the criterion that a film should promote, or at least not damage, psychological health. Notice the qualifying word "children's" in "children's movies." Is the author saying that Disney films damage only children, or that other kinds of movies are psychologically damaging but Disney takes the top prize for damaging effects among children's films? I tend to think the latter.

14 The argument of many an exhausted parent... the phrase "the happiest place on earth" is, of course, Disney's own marketing tagline. I'm not sure why Disney in particular came in for a thumping in my classes.

15 This one is going to take some patient work in both describing the two phenomena (a liberal education and a practically based one) and setting up the criteria for a good education. I would think some serious definitional work would be involved, but probably also causal work, showing that the effects of a liberal education are better than the effects of a practically based one.

16 I like the contrast here with the previous thesis, as this one will surely deal with almost entirely technical and even statistical evidence: survival rates, rates of complications, rates of secondary infections, etc. It's good to show that evaluative arguments are made over matters that have statistical evidence. Then again, this thesis might come down to questions about postoperative quality of life and thus deal with questions not reducible to statistical or technical evidence.

17 You may remember the causal thesis about extroverts and introverts in the churches. I was pleased to see the student use this topic as she explored each of the Four Arguments, so I include it here to show how she developed her argument and explored the topic more fully as she worked through stasis theory. (Watch for this topic to surface again in the next chapter.)

18 Encourage your students not to shortchange this stage because evaluative arguments require so many judgment calls vis-à-vis topic, intention, and audience. If students can work out these questions at this stage, it will allow the actual drafting of the paper to be much more productive. Help them to see that this stage, too, is a valuable and important part of "writing."

19 It would be good to come back to this again and again as the students learn the Four Arguments: It helps them become better, more intelligent, and more critical readers of others' arguments.

20 I hope that this speech is at least somewhat familiar to your students, but I realize that some of them might be reading it for the first time. I have not provided notes on the vocabulary here that might seem obscure ("bare bodkin" comes to mind, or "contumely"), hoping that you will have an edition you can use as you take them through the soliloquy. If this is the students' first encounter with the speech, you might want to provide some of the context, but it actually works quite well as a meditation on life even for students who don't know the sea of troubles Hamlet is facing at this point in the play. The discussion, I hope, will lead the students to see that Hamlet quickly drops the question of which is nobler. He implies, but does not lay out, criteria for deciding whether something is noble or not. And he concludes without finding any way to discover noble action whatsoever—at least at this point in the play.

CHAPTER FOUR

1 If you have been using your own example instead of the bar fight to work through these chapters, by all means use it. I return to it to show how stasis theory leads us from the beginning of an issue all the way through to practical action about it.

2 I wanted to review the whole purpose of stasis theory here at the end, and I hope you will do so with your students. I find that it really helps to cement the process in their minds if they can see each part, each kind of argument, in relation to the whole.

At the end of the chapter, I will, in a qualified way, question this optimistic view of arguing and of human nature. When you get there, you might return to these sentences at the beginning of the chapter and discuss with your students how the study of argumentation leads one to consider a fundamental view of human nature.

3 It might be helpful to work through a couple of other issues in this way, giving students practice moving from definitional to policy arguments. You might choose an important national issue such as gun control, or a local school issue, or even a lighthearted one from family life.

4 I encourage you to have a class brainstorming session where you come up with even more topics. It might help to give students parameters: national problems, school problems, local problems. Or change the subject matter: economic and financial problems, moral problems, psychological problems, etc. The more students see that they already engage in these arguments, the more interesting the discussion will become. You might choose

to use a few of their topics as you work through this chapter instead of the ones I have included.

5 Here you could return to the list of topics the class brainstormed and see which ones fit in each of these categories. If the students do not agree whether or not a problem is well known, that itself is great—it makes my next point for me.

6 I hope this section provides a helpful review of the other kinds of arguments so your students can use them effectively long after the course is complete. If you like, you could have them practice by doing this with two or three other topics. You might break the class into groups, assign each a different topic, and have them report back in five to seven minutes how they would use the other three arguments to help them describe the problem.

7 Because of this need for research, you should budget time for the students to produce good problem/solution arguments. Perhaps you could have the students explore the topic for a while and then turn in a detailed outline. As you critique the outline, you can suggest areas for further research. Then you can allow time for that work to take place before the final version of the paper is due.

8 Because some of these concrete proposals are more immediately controversial than arguments in the other three chapters, I have chosen to present them as pro/con pairs.

9 This is often a place for teacher intervention: helping the students focus a solution so that it will be specific, clear, concrete, and actionable. Group work can help, as students can evaluate one another's thesis statements for these three qualities. But you may have to help students yourself, and now is the time to do so.

10 Taking the students through these four tasks is the crucial work of this chapter. Many students don't immediately see all of the tasks. Or if they do see, they don't realize how important they are. Or if they do realize how important they are, they don't know how to execute the four tasks. But working with the students to take on these tasks, and thus argue for their solution, is essential here. Do not slight this process. Give it time and get the students to work through each of the four in turn.

11 I cannot emphasize enough how much students gloss over the whole topic of feasibility. A great part of it is inexperience, but below I suggest there might be a larger reason. At any rate, it is crucial to question them on all the details of feasibility for their projects. They do not know what things cost, which is understandable, but they often do not consider the need for proper human resources either.

12 Students know that others have proposed solutions, but often they do not realize how much they need to engage with these other solutions as they propose their own. A good way to do this is to engage them in recounting some family debate, where one sibling has proposed doing one thing (going to an art museum) and another has proposed doing something different (going to a sporting event). They quickly realize they have already argued in this way many times.

13 There are, of course, plenty of other categories of concerns not yet addressed: social, cultural, psychological, etc. You might bring some of these categories to the discussion. I mention aesthetic concerns (which students rarely consider) and ethical ones (which students often consider) simply to show how the four categories above do not in any way exhaust the critiques a proposal might face.
14 You and your students might notice that I have not discussed this; I save it for my mini-essay at the end of the chapter.
15 Students are often quite interested in this topic, and because it encourages interesting research into history, the psychobiology of circadian rhythms, and more, it can produce some interesting papers.
16 Again, this is a marvelous topic for thoughtful research of various types—scientific papers, in-person interviews, government materials, etc. Later I will address the problem of incentivization with this thesis.
17 This is another complex issue that will require research and a prudent balancing of conflicting goods.
18 I hope this final mini-essay—the last section of the entire Four Arguments core of the book—provides an overview of what I am trying to achieve and offers a kind of anthropology that makes sense of what it means to argue and what is necessary for the rhetor to know, acknowledge, and develop in his own soul. If it's not to your taste, feel free to omit it from your own teaching. But I hope you will read it yourself, so you know what I'm trying to accomplish.
19 I could not resist including Swift's wickedly brilliant argument, and I hope you will enjoy breaking it down with your students. I find that this essay, which used to be common in anthologies, is not featured as often in today's course materials, so you may have the delight of having many of your students read it for the first time—and even have some students who read it "straight" and come to class angry at Swift, thinking that he seriously proposes such a barbaric solution. But the real good for our purposes here is using this essay to cement the tasks of a good problem/solution argument in their minds by showing how artfully Swift accomplishes every task we have been studying—and does it deadpan.
20 I urge you to work through this argument with your students—after, that is, allowing them to read it through once by themselves; the shock of a first-time read is one of the real delights of encountering Swift's savage satire. Have students mark out the parts of a problem/solution argument. Swift lays out the problem clearly, articulates his solution, shows in mathematical detail (this is one of the delights of the piece) how his solution is feasible, shows how it is better than other solutions, and handles other counterarguments. He even suggests the incentives that will encourage poor Irish parents to take up this solution! As with the other classic texts, I have elected not to clutter the text with footnotes, hoping that, as you work through the essay with your students, you will want to judge how much of this information to impart to them. There are plenty of websites and other resources that can supply information such as who the Pretender was, how much a shilling is, and more.

Many students miss that Swift cleverly smuggles in his own solutions to these seemingly intractable problems five paragraphs from the end, in the paragraph beginning "I can think of no one objection," disguised as his dismissal of other possible solutions. Taken as a whole, the solutions seem fascinatingly prudent and practical, and his savage rejection of them in the next paragraph belies Swift's actual thoughts on the problem of poverty in Ireland as well as his anger at the authorities and the upper class for not pursuing these solutions. A reader might have guessed this earlier, however, from his suggestion that idle young women would actually be a better meal than Catholic infants: "Neither indeed can I deny, that if the same use were made of several plump young girls in this town, who without one single groat to their fortunes, cannot stir abroad without a chair, and appear at a playhouse and assemblies in foreign fineries which they never will pay for, the kingdom would not be the worse."

I will note that you might want to discuss with the students how Swift, who is beloved by the Irish to this day for his defense of them, has his speaker traffic in the most common and hurtful stereotypes about the Irish, especially Catholic Irish. (Swift was dean of the Anglican St. Patrick's Cathedral in Dublin.) You will perhaps want to talk about the speaker's casual antisemitism as well.

CHAPTER FIVE

1 I encourage students to ask the question, "What does all this matter in the real world?" We should always have answer to that question—not to turn every subject toward some immediate practical benefit but so that students can see that learning of any kind can lead to a life well lived. In this chapter, I aim to show students that mastering the Four Arguments will have proximate and remote benefits.

2 I hope you will have some time to discuss these two senses of the word "discipline" with your students, talk about how discipline leads to habit, and even examine the close connection between the words "habit" and "virtue." These words are loaded with negative connotations, and transforming these into positive ones is an incredibly important part of a liberal education.

3 Often students, especially students who love science and wish to major in it, do need to have this pointed out—that scientific papers are precisely that, arguments. I have often argued (there's that word again) that if we taught science as a series of arguments made—some of them successful, others not (see Darwin versus Lamarck), we could both demonstrate the human drama of science and its often contentious nature and draw more students in to the fascinating enterprise of trying to articulate to others one's attempts to understand the world around us. You might take one such moment in the history of science—Copernicus and the heliocentric universe, for example—and show that this scientist really did put forward an argument, and it had to win the day. It's not that people before Copernicus were stupid; they had a coherent model of the universe that (largely)

fit the data. Copernicus had to argue that his model actually fit the data better, that it was a better explanation of well-known phenomena than the popular one.

4 I list and explore only these particular fields below, but of course the examples are endless, and you should feel free to explore the fields you know best or align with your students' interests. If you have a class full of musicians, or engineers, or cricket players, use that to your pedagogical advantage.

5 If you like, you might return to that quiz with your class, or invent a new version of it, and give it to the students. My students are often amazed at how easy it is now, how much progress they have made, how second-nature the Four Arguments have become to them. Their confidence soars.

6 I'm not pulling anyone's leg here; I honestly didn't know what I was doing as a literary critic—at least in terms of stasis theory. And this was strange to me, because I was in graduate school in the 1980s, when literary theory was the highest of high arts and when explorations of what literary criticism is and does were the coin of the realm. I went on to teach literary theory many times. And yet this question puzzled me to no end: What sort of argument am I making when I interpret *Beowulf*? I won't say it created an existential crisis, but it did make me wonder how to fit together these two parts of my academic life.

7 If your students have not read the *Iliad*, it seems to me you have two choices. You can either give them a quick overview of the poem so that they understand this next section of the chapter or you can take what I am doing here and adapt it to a work of literature your students have read, using a prompt from your own curriculum. The concepts are the same whether you are working from Jane Austen or James Joyce or Toni Morrison. The same is true for the *Beowulf* example below. You won't hurt my feelings if you go off script here!